Michael Turner

When the Dragons Return
An Esoteric Guide to the New Age

Original Title: *When the Dragons Return – An Esoteric Guide for the New Age*
Copyright © 2025, published by Luiz Antonio dos Santos ME.
This book is a non-fiction work that explores practices and concepts in the field of esotericism and spiritual awakening. Through a comprehensive approach, the author offers insights into elemental forces, consciousness, and the spiritual return of dragons as archetypes and energies of transformation.
1st Edition
Production Team
Author: Michael Turner
Editor: Luiz Santos
Cover: Studios Booklas / *Eli Moonridge*
Consultant: *Jasper Helman*
Researchers: *Naomi Kells, Dorian Haan, Lucas Virel*
Layout: *Arin Goldwell*

Publication and Identification
When the Dragons Return
Booklas, 2025
Categories: Esotericism / Spirituality
DDC: 133.93 — **CDU**: 133.5

All rights reserved to:
Luiz Antonio dos Santos ME / Booklas
No part of this book may be reproduced, stored in a retrieval system, or transmitted in any form — electronic, mechanical, photocopying, recording, or otherwise — without the prior written permission of the copyright holder.

Sumário

Sustematic Index 5
Foreword 11
Chapter 1 What Are Dragons? 14
Chapter 2 Dragons in History and Mythology 20
Chapter 3 Dragons in Esotericism and Spirituality 25
Chapter 4 Why Did They Leave? 31
Chapter 5 The Return of the Dragons 37
Chapter 6 The Dragons and the Four Elements 42
Chapter 7 Dragons of Fire 48
Chapter 8 Water Dragons 53
Chapter 9 Earth Dragons 58
Chapter 10 Dragons of Air 63
Chapter 11 The Spiritual Awakening and the Dragons 69
Chapter 12 Energy Portals 75
Chapter 13 Connecting with Dragons 85
Chapter 14 Dragons as Spiritual Guardians 92
Chapter 15 Evolution of Consciousness 99
Chapter 16 Dragons and Kundalini Energy 105
Chapter 17 Dragons and the Protection of the Planet 112
Chapter 18 Dragons in Magic and Rituals 119
Chapter 19 Encounters with Dragons 126
Chapter 20 The Draconic Bloodlines 132
Chapter 21 Guardians of the Timelines 138
Chapter 22 Interdimensional Dragons and the Multiverse 145
Chapter 23 Dragons in the New Age 151

Chapter 24 Meditations with Dragons 157
Chapter 25 Invocations and Energy Circles............................ 163
Chapter 26 How to Honor the Dragons 169
Chapter 27 Messages from the Unconscious 174
Chapter 28 Personal Development... 179
Chapter 29 How to Sense the Presence of Dragons................ 184
Chapter 30 The Masters and Guardians.................................. 189
Chapter 31 The Final Calling... 193
Epilogue 198

Sustematic Index

Capítulo 1: What Are Dragons? - Explores the profound archetypes represented by dragons across cultures and ages, symbolizing primordial forces that influence the world and human existence.

Capítulo 2: Dragons in History and Mythology - Examines the enigmatic presence of dragons in diverse mythologies and cultures throughout history, reflecting humanity's relationship with the unknown.

Capítulo 3: Dragons in Esotericism and Spirituality - Discusses the manifestation of dragons as a living force in spirituality and esotericism, recognized as guardians of ancestral knowledge and interdimensional consciousnesses.

Capítulo 4: Why Did They Leave? - Investigates the mystery behind the apparent disappearance of dragons from human reality, exploring esoteric theories about their withdrawal to higher dimensions or concealment due to humanity's spiritual decline.

Capítulo 5: The Return of the Dragons - Addresses the prophecy of the dragons' return, linking it to planetary transformation, the elevation of human consciousness, and the restoration of Earth's energetic balance.

Capítulo 6: The Dragons and the Four Elements - Explores the connection between dragons and the fundamental elements of the universe, fire, water, earth, and air, and how they act as guardians and catalysts of these energies.

Capítulo 7: Dragons of Fire - Focuses on the transformative energy of fire dragons, representing the principle of creation and destruction, the driving force of evolution, and the awakening of consciousness.

Capítulo 8: Water Dragons - Centers on water dragons as guardians of emotional flow and ancestral knowledge, embodying fluidity, intuition, and the power to navigate life's natural cycles.

Capítulo 9: Earth Dragons - Highlights earth dragons as embodiments of solidity, resilience, and the deep connection to primordial forces, teaching the importance of patience, constancy, and building strong foundations.

Capítulo 10: Dragons of Air - Centers on air dragons as embodiments of freedom, wisdom, and the expansion of consciousness, acting as messengers of cosmic knowledge and inspiring clarity of thought.

Capítulo 11: The Spiritual Awakening and the Dragons - Explores the connection between dragons and the human journey of self-discovery, portraying them as powerful allies in the awakening of consciousness and spiritual ascension.

Capítulo 12: Energy Portals - Discusses the Earth's network of energy flows and the role of dragons as guardians of these energy portals, acting as points of convergence between telluric and cosmic forces.

Capítulo 13: Connecting with Dragons - Focuses on the subtle nature of connecting with dragons, emphasizing the importance of developing sensitivity, receptivity, and respect to perceive their presence and establish a meaningful bond.

Capítulo 14: Dragons as Spiritual Guardians - Explores the role of dragons as spiritual guardians in esoteric traditions, representing a higher consciousness that protects, guides, and challenges individuals on the path of spiritual evolution.

Capítulo 15: Evolution of Consciousness - Discusses the role of dragons in the continuous process of human consciousness evolution, symbolizing the forces that test and guide individuals toward higher states of perception.

Capítulo 16: Dragons and Kundalini Energy - Explores the connection between dragons and Kundalini energy, representing the powerful forces of transformation and hidden potential within human beings.

Capítulo 17: Dragons and the Protection of the Planet - Focuses on the role of dragons in maintaining the harmony of the environment and the Earth's energy flows, acting as guardians of nature and protectors of the planet.

Capítulo 18: Dragons in Magic and Rituals - Discusses dragon magic as a path of profound power and transformation, highlighting the role of dragons as guardians of hidden knowledge and primordial energies.

Capítulo 19: Encounters with Dragons - Explores the nature of encounters with dragons on the spiritual plane, describing them as profound experiences that occur in expanded states of consciousness and serve as catalysts for self-discovery and transformation.

Capítulo 20: The Draconic Bloodlines - Centers on draconic bloodlines as a spiritual inheritance, representing a deep energetic resonance with dragons, rooted in ancestral memories and vibrational patterns that influence individuals' character and life mission.

Capítulo 21: Guardians of the Timelines - Explores the connection between dragons and time, portraying them as guardians of interdimensional passages who protect the balance of timelines and ensure the harmonious flow of events.

Capítulo 22: Interdimensional Dragons and the Multiverse - Focuses on interdimensional dragons as cosmic travelers who traverse different planes of existence and interact with multiple realities, possessing an advanced understanding of the laws governing the structure of reality.

Capítulo 23: Dragons in the New Age - Explores the resurgence of draconic energy in the New Age as a powerful presence influencing the expansion of human perception, the awakening of ancient knowledge, and the acceleration of spiritual ascension.

Capítulo 24: Meditations with Dragons - Focuses on dragon meditation as a practice to access the energy and wisdom of these ancestral entities, requiring alignment of mind, body, and spirit to establish a genuine connection.

Capítulo 25: Invocations and Energy Circles - Centers on connecting with dragons through invocations and energy circles, emphasizing the importance of preparation, energetic alignment, and creating a sacred space for this interaction.

Capítulo 26: How to Honor the Dragons - Provides guidance on honoring dragons, emphasizing that it involves more than rituals, requiring an inner alignment with their values, such as courage, wisdom, loyalty, and transformation.

Capítulo 27: Messages from the Unconscious - Explores the significance of dragons in dreams as messages from the unconscious, representing challenges, protection, power, and wisdom, and their role in self-discovery and personal transformation.

Capítulo 28: Personal Development - Centers on personal development fueled by the energy of dragons, describing it as a transformative journey that awakens inner strength, challenges limits, and guides individuals in discovering their true potential.

Capítulo 29: How to Sense the Presence of Dragons - Provides guidance on sensing the presence of dragons in the spiritual realm, highlighting the importance of heightened sensitivity, recognizing subtle signs, and being open to experiences that defy everyday logic.

Capítulo 30: The Masters and Guardians - Focuses on dragons as spiritual masters and guardians, representing a higher consciousness that guides those willing to face challenges and seek wisdom on their evolutionary journey.

Capítulo 31: The Final Calling - Centers on the transformative nature of connecting with dragons, emphasizing that it is a challenge that demands readiness, courage, and a willingness to embrace change and self-discovery.

Foreword

With great conviction, I present to readers a seminal work for understanding one of humanity's most enduring mysteries: dragons. Far from the superficial fantasies that populate the popular imagination, this book reveals the true nature of these majestic beings, unveiling their crucial role in the energetic balance of our planet and in our own spiritual evolution.

Since time immemorial, the figure of the dragon has echoed in the mythologies of cultures scattered across the globe, even those that have never had contact with one another. This universality is no mere coincidence. It attests to an ancestral reality, a profound knowledge that resides in the core of our collective consciousness. The winged serpent Quetzalcoatl, the celestial dragons of China, the fearsome Leviathan, and the European guardians of treasures are distinct manifestations of the same primordial truth: dragons are elemental beings, forces of nature personified, intrinsically linked to our spiritual health.

Dragons are much more than inventions of fantasy. They are beings of high vibrational frequency, elemental entities that have shared our planet for ages. The holistic view presented here demonstrates that humanity's growing estrangement from its own spiritual essence, our disconnection from nature, and the relentless pursuit of empty materialism have created an energetic dissonance that has made our world inhospitable to these creatures of pure energy. It was this disconnection that led to their departure from our plane of existence.

However, the author, with profound knowledge and sensitivity, reveals that we are in a moment of crucial transition. The awakening of a new spiritual consciousness in various sectors of society, the renewed interest in nature, and the search for a higher purpose in life are gradually restoring the vibrational harmony of our planet. And with this restoration comes the strong conviction, supported by growing evidence and intuition, that the dragons are returning.

It is essential to understand that an encounter with a true dragon does not resemble the cinematic depictions of epic battles against scaly beasts. Dragons, in their elemental nature, manifest primarily on the energetic and spiritual plane. The experiences of those who have felt their presence are diverse and profound: sensations of intense heat, waves of vibrant energy, an imposing and protective presence, revealing dreams, clear intuitions, and the perception of symbols laden with meaning.

These beings are not mere guardians of material treasures, but rather guardians of ancestral wisdom and bearers of immense transformative power. Their return is not a threat, but a call. An invitation for humanity to rekindle its spiritual flame, to restore balance with the web of life, and to embrace a future of greater awareness and harmony.

This book is not a vague theory, but a clear and affirmative exposition on the true nature of dragons. The author, with his deep understanding of the subject, presents evidence and insights that prove the existence of these elemental beings and their vital role in our evolutionary journey. By demystifying the distorted image perpetuated by popular culture, this work offers a new perspective, inviting the reader to open their mind and heart to a reality far richer and more mysterious than they ever imagined.

If you have always felt an inexplicable connection to dragons, if deep intuitions have guided you to this book, or if you simply seek a deeper understanding of the forces that shape our world, then you are ready to receive the truth revealed here. Prepare for a journey of discovery that will make you see the world – and yourself – in a new light.

With the certainty that this work will transform your perception,

Luiz Santos Editor

Chapter 1
What Are Dragons?

Dragons are more than mere creatures of fantasy; they represent profound archetypes that transcend cultures and ages, symbolizing primordial forces that influence the world and human existence itself. At their core, they embody the duality of destruction and creation, chaos and order, challenge and enlightenment. From the earliest civilizations, their stories have intertwined with the myths of gods, heroes, and sages, suggesting that their presence extends far beyond the purely mythological. Some see them as physical beings that once walked among humans, while others understand them as energetic manifestations, guardians of ancestral knowledge, and bearers of hidden truths. Their depictions vary widely, but they always carry a sense of immeasurable power and unfathomable mystery, reinforcing the idea that they are not just imaginary figures, but symbols that resonate with fundamental aspects of the human journey.

Throughout history, dragons have been described in distinct ways, depending on the culture recording them. In the West, their image has largely been associated with terror and destruction, portrayed as colossal beasts that breathe fire and devastate entire kingdoms. Many medieval legends place them as obstacles to be overcome by brave knights, reinforcing the metaphor of confronting one's own fears and limitations. In the East, however, particularly in Chinese and Japanese traditions, dragons are revered as benevolent entities, connected to natural forces and universal balance. They are seen as wise beings, bringers of fortune and protection, influencing harvests, rivers, and even the destiny of nations. These differences reflect not only distinct views of the unknown, but also the way each civilization faced the challenges of existence and the role of the forces that govern the cosmos.

Beyond legends and mythological interpretations, many esoteric and spiritual traditions consider dragons as entities that transcend physicality, existing in subtle dimensions and interacting with those who are prepared to understand their energy. They are described as guardians of sacred knowledge, protectors of dimensional portals, and allies of those who seek truth beyond appearances. This view attributes to dragons a function far beyond the mythical figure of colossal beasts, placing them in a context of spiritual transformation and connection with higher forces. The relationship between humans and dragons, in this sense, is not one of domination or submission, but of learning and evolution. Those who allow themselves to understand their presence gain access to a profound wisdom, capable of illuminating paths and revealing truths that remain hidden to most.

Mythology and folklore describe them as immense beings, often winged, with resistant scales, sharp claws, and eyes that carry the intensity of an eternal flame. In the West, the most common image is that of the fire-breathing dragon, a symbol of power and destruction. In the East, especially in China and Japan, dragons are celestial beings, associated with fortune, wisdom, and the balance of natural forces. These contrasts reveal something essential: dragons are not just mythological figures, but archetypal representations of primordial forces that humanity has always sought to understand.

In esoteric and holistic circles, dragons are seen as conscious energies, holders of ancestral knowledge, and guardians of interdimensional portals. They do not belong solely to the material plane, but transit between dimensions, influencing events and individuals when necessary. It is believed that those who can tune into their energy can access hidden information, spiritual protection, and an inner power that transcends common understanding.

Ancient civilizations recorded stories that suggest real encounters with these beings. In Mesopotamian traditions, the goddess Tiamat, described as a primordial dragon, symbolized the primordial chaos that preceded the creation of the world. In Hindu scriptures, the cosmic serpent Ananta Shesha supports the universe and serves as Vishnu's throne, representing supreme order. In Scandinavia, the figure of the dragon Nidhogg appears as an entity that gnaws at the roots of the

Yggdrasil tree, connecting to the idea of cycles of destruction and renewal.

Many of these narratives speak not only of physical entities, but of cosmic forces at work in existence. Dragons can be understood as symbols of transformation, transmutation, and spiritual elevation. Those who connect with their energy learn to deal with their own challenges, overcome fears, and expand consciousness beyond the limitations imposed by the material world.

In the holistic view, dragons represent the fundamental elements of nature. Each one manifests in a distinct energetic frequency, influencing not only the surrounding reality, but also the way people interact with their own emotions and internal challenges. The presence of a fire dragon, for example, brings the force of transmutation, burning away what no longer serves and driving personal growth. Water dragons flow with intuition and sensitivity, aiding connection with the unconscious and emotional clarity. Earth dragons support and protect, providing stability and structure. Air dragons expand the mind, fostering communication and connection with higher dimensions.

Many spiritual lineages affirm that dragons never left Earth, but merely retreated to more subtle planes, awaiting the right moment to manifest again. With humanity's current spiritual awakening, some people report intense dreams with dragons, visions during meditative states, and even energetic experiences that indicate a rapprochement. In some traditions, it is believed that dragons only present themselves to those who are ready to receive their teachings, as their power cannot be treated lightly.

Draconic guardians do not serve human whims, nor do they respond to banal invocations. They appear when the soul is prepared, when there is a real purpose for evolution, and when the established connection aims at genuine growth. This relationship is not one of domination, but of mutual learning. The person who connects with a dragon experiences a process of profound transformation, as their presence illuminates hidden truths and challenges all that is illusory.

The tradition that dragons guard treasures is a powerful metaphor within esotericism. The gold they protect is not physical, but represents hidden knowledge, the supreme truth that few are able to access. To reach this treasure, one must go through trials, confront one's own shadows, and demonstrate courage in the face of the unknown. The dragon does not give its wisdom to those who seek shortcuts or easy rewards. Only those truly committed to their spiritual journey can cross the threshold of its presence.

The ancients knew that dragons represented much more than mythical beasts. In various cultures, kings, emperors, and shamans sought their blessing and guidance. In the East, Chinese emperors declared themselves descendants of the dragon, which gave them divine authority and wisdom. In the West, the knights who faced dragons symbolized the fight against their own fears and limitations. In indigenous tribes, the winged serpent was seen as an ancestral spirit that guided initiates through the mysteries of existence.

Those who feel a calling to understand dragons in the holistic context need to delve into their symbolism, but, more than that, they must learn to feel their presence. Contact with these energies does not occur only through the rational mind, but through sensitive perception and surrender to the process of spiritual connection. Some practices can facilitate this approach, such as focused meditation, the study of natural elements, and the pursuit of self-knowledge.

Dragons represent the beginning and the end, chaos and order, mystery and revelation. They exist in a frequency beyond common understanding, but they make themselves present to those who truly wish to tread the path of wisdom. At the right time, they manifest, guiding those who are ready to awaken to a reality far greater than what the eyes can see.

Chapter 2
Dragons in History and Mythology

Since the dawn of humanity, dragons have emerged as enigmatic symbols, transcending cultures and civilizations that had no contact with one another. The recurring presence of these creatures in such diverse mythologies raises intriguing questions: are they merely products of the collective imagination, or remnants of something deeper, a shared ancestral memory? The way they have been portrayed has varied widely, but their presence has always been linked to fundamental forces of the universe, whether as agents of destruction, guardians of wisdom, or cosmic entities balancing order and chaos. Their significance has transcended time, influencing everything from the earliest scriptures to modern myths, demonstrating that dragons are not just mythical beings, but powerful representations of the human relationship with the unknown.

The earliest civilizations left records depicting dragons as primordial figures, associated with the beginning of creation and the structuring of the cosmos. In Mesopotamian, Egyptian, and Hindu cultures, colossal dragons and serpents personified both primordial chaos and eternal wisdom. These entities were seen as living forces that shaped reality, and their presence in myths was not casual: they represented the link between the spiritual and material realms, influencing everything from the balance of natural forces to human destinies. In some traditions, dragons were beings of challenge, demanding courage and sacrifice from those who sought to overcome them; in others, they were revered as sources of power and knowledge, accessible only to those worthy of their presence.

Regardless of the form they took throughout the ages, dragons remained symbols of hidden power and transformation. Their representations range from demonized beings in Western traditions to celestial deities in Eastern mythology, revealing that their essence has always reflected the values and beliefs of the societies that evoked them. When we analyze the stories and myths that surround them, we realize that dragons are not just fantastic creatures, but profound archetypes that continue to influence the human psyche and spiritual understanding. The search for their true meaning goes beyond mythology, connecting to the mystery of existence and the human desire to understand the invisible forces that govern the world.

In Mesopotamia, one of humanity's earliest written records, we find the myth of the goddess Tiamat. Represented as a colossal dragon, Tiamat symbolized the primordial chaos from which the world was generated. Her battle against Marduk, the god of order, became a metaphor for the balance between creation and destruction, an idea that would be repeated in other mythologies. The figure of the dragon as a chaotic and powerful being, often fought by a heroic deity, became ingrained in various later cultures.

In Ancient Egypt, Apep (Apophis), the serpent of chaos, threatened to devour the sun during its nightly journey through the underworld. Only the strength of Ra, the sun god, kept this draconic entity under control. The constant battle between Ra and Apep represented the eternal cycle of day and night, order and chaos, demonstrating that dragons were associated with fundamental cosmic aspects.

In the Hindu tradition, the figure of the Nagas stands out. These serpentine beings, often described as half-human, half-dragon, are considered guardians of wisdom and sacred rivers. The cosmic serpent Ananta Shesha, upon whom Vishnu rests, represents eternity and the sustenance of the universe. Unlike Western narratives, where dragons are often antagonists, in Vedic culture they assume a role of balance and protection.

Chinese mythology elevated dragons to a celestial level, making them symbols of wisdom, prosperity, and divine authority. Unlike Western representations, Chinese dragons were not necessarily winged, but serpentine, and governed the natural elements. The Azure Dragon ruled over waters and rains, revered by emperors who sought to maintain climatic harmony in their realms. In temples and festivals, the presence of dragons symbolized luck and renewal, reinforcing the belief that they were benevolent beings, indispensable for cosmic order.

The Nordic peoples had a darker view of dragons, often associating them with destruction and greed.

Nidhogg, one of the most feared, gnawed at the roots of Yggdrasil, the world tree, threatening the balance of the universe. The presence of dragons like Fafnir, whose greed transformed him into an evil monster, reinforced the idea that these beings represented challenges for heroes, being symbols of the temptations and obstacles of the spiritual journey.

In the Christian tradition, the dragon took on a demonized role. Medieval iconography often depicted St. George defeating a dragon, a symbol of the victory of faith over the forces of evil. The Book of Revelation describes Satan as a great red dragon, emphasizing the idea that these creatures were associated with danger and heresy. This interpretation contrasted sharply with the Eastern view, where dragons were honored and respected.

The indigenous cultures of the Americas also had accounts of winged serpents and dragons. The Aztecs venerated Quetzalcoatl, the feathered serpent, as a creator god and benevolent being, responsible for the transmission of knowledge and civilization. The Maya had the figure of Kukulkan, a similar deity, who also ruled the heavens and waters. These draconic entities were associated with fertility and renewal, showing a more spiritualized approach to the subject.

If dragons were merely mythological inventions, why would they appear in such distant cultures, with such similar characteristics? Some esoteric scholars believe that dragons may have been real beings, present in ancient times, and that their withdrawal from the physical plane gave rise to these legends. Others argue that dragons represent archetypes of the human unconscious, manifesting as symbols of inner strength and the path of personal evolution.

What is clear is that dragons played a crucial role in the construction of the worldview of ancient peoples. Whether seen as guardians, adversaries, or deities, their presence influenced religions, rituals, and the very structure of myths. The way they were understood varied according to culture, but their profound meaning remained: dragons symbolize latent power, hidden knowledge, and transformation.

Many modern occultists and scholars try to rescue the true essence of dragons, freeing them from the distortions and fears propagated by later cultural and religious influences. In some contemporary spiritual traditions, there is an effort to reconnect with the draconic energy, seeking to understand what these entities represented for the ancients and how their wisdom can be applied in the awakening of human consciousness.

The story of dragons does not belong only to the past. Their influences can still be felt today, whether in the symbolism of dreams, in spiritual practices, or in the search for a deeper understanding of reality. Understanding the multiple facets of dragons throughout history allows us to see beyond conventional representations, accessing an ancestral knowledge that can reveal forgotten truths about humanity's own path.

Chapter 3
Dragons in Esotericism and Spirituality

The presence of dragons in spirituality and esotericism transcends the boundaries of legends and mythologies, manifesting as a living force that influences the human journey on subtle and profound levels. In various occult traditions, these beings are recognized as guardians of ancestral knowledge, holders of a wisdom that dates back to the origin of the cosmos. For many students of the occult, dragons are not merely symbolic figures, but interdimensional consciousnesses that interact with those who demonstrate the spiritual maturity to access their energy. Their connection with the elements of nature, with the cycles of transformation, and with the mysteries of the universe makes them powerful entities, capable of assisting in personal development and the expansion of consciousness. Those who seek to understand their true essence realize that dragons represent a call to self-knowledge, challenging individuals to confront their shadows and transcend them.

Throughout history, different esoteric schools and spiritual traditions have associated dragons with primordial forces of transmutation and evolution. In Alchemy, for example, the dragon symbolizes the process of purification and rebirth, being a fundamental archetype in the search for the Philosopher's Stone. The Ouroboros, represented by a dragon or serpent devouring its own tail, expresses the cyclical nature of existence, the fusion between beginning and end, the dissolution of the ego, and the integration of the self with the whole. In Hermeticism, dragons are seen as protectors of occult knowledge, ensuring that only those who are prepared can access the secrets of creation. Many mystical orders describe dragons as beings that operate on higher planes, guiding those who demonstrate discipline, respect, and understanding of their energetic nature.

Connection with dragons can occur in various ways, whether through revealing dreams, visions during meditative states, or energetic experiences that evidence their presence. Some magical traditions use specific rituals to establish a link with these entities, evoking their energy for protection, guidance, and spiritual strengthening. In shamanic practices, dragons are considered ancestral spirits that aid in healing, the transition between dimensions, and the harmony between body, mind, and spirit. The awakening of draconic energy, however, does not occur randomly or superficially: it requires commitment, courage, and an open heart to understand the transformations that these beings can bring. When connecting with a dragon, the practitioner begins a journey of self-discovery, where illusions are dissolved and profound truths are revealed. It is a path of power, but also of great responsibility, reserved for those who are ready to tread a path of genuine evolution.

Throughout history, mystery schools and occult societies have described dragons as interdimensional entities, possessing a wisdom that dates back to the dawn of creation. Some traditions maintain that dragons are not merely mythological figures, but living consciousnesses that reside in subtle planes and manifest to those who possess the necessary vibration to interact with their energy. This view suggests that dragons did not depart from Earth, but merely withdrew from human eyes, awaiting the moment when humanity is ready to receive their teachings again.

In the studies of Alchemy, dragons are frequently represented as symbols of transformation and transmutation. The figure of the dragon devouring its own tail, known as the Ouroboros, represents the eternal cycle of life, death, and rebirth. This symbol is used to illustrate the cyclical nature of existence and the process of spiritual evolution that every seeker must undergo. The alchemical dragon is also associated with the inner flame that consumes the impurities of the being, allowing the true essence to manifest.

In the tradition of Hermeticism, dragons are described as guardians of sacred knowledge, keeping the hidden wisdom out of reach of those who are not prepared to receive it. Many esoteric texts warn that attempting to access this knowledge without preparation can lead to destruction, as the energy of dragons is intense and transformative. Only those who demonstrate discipline, humility, and courage can cross the portals that lead to the understanding of their mysteries.

In Shamanism, dragons are seen as ancestral spirits that help practitioners navigate between worlds. In some indigenous cultures, the winged serpent represents supreme wisdom and connection with the heavens. Shamans who communicate with these energies report that dragons teach about the balance of the elements and the harmony between body, mind, and spirit. Contact with these forces requires respect and commitment, as dragons do not respond to banal invocations or selfish requests.

In the context of subtle energies, dragons are also associated with the four elements of nature. Each type of dragon vibrates at a specific frequency and manifests a corresponding energy:

Fire dragons are symbols of power, transmutation, and courage. They aid in awakening inner strength and destroying limiting patterns.

Water dragons work with emotional fluidity, intuition, and healing. Their energy is gentle yet profound, helping to dissolve internal blockages.

Earth dragons offer protection and stability, connecting those who seek security and structure in their spiritual journey.

Air dragons expand consciousness and promote mental clarity, communication with higher planes, and understanding of occult knowledge.

Connection with dragons can manifest in various ways. Some people report encounters with these entities in dreams, where dragons appear as guides who convey messages or teach important lessons. Others feel their presence during meditative states, perceiving images, thermal sensations, or intense energetic vibrations. There are also those who channel their energy during rituals, using specific symbols, mantras, and visualizations to establish a deeper contact.

One of the most common spiritual practices for connecting with dragons is guided meditation. In this process, the practitioner enters a state of deep relaxation and visualizes a dragon appearing in their energy field. The goal is not to control or command the creature, but rather to be receptive to what it wishes to convey. Communication with dragons occurs intuitively, through sensory impressions, mental images, or even telepathic messages.

Dragons also appear in various magical traditions. In some branches of ceremonial magic, they are evoked as guardians of interdimensional portals or as allies in works of protection and energetic strengthening. In Druidism and pagan practices, dragons are linked to the primordial forces of the Earth and can be honored through natural rituals. Some esoteric orders use specific sigils and runes to invoke their presence and obtain spiritual guidance.

The return of dragons to collective consciousness is seen by many spiritualists as a sign of the planet's vibrational shift. Some say that these beings are manifesting again because humanity is awakening to a new level of consciousness. The elevation of planetary energy would make more direct contact with dragons possible, allowing their messages and teachings to be understood more clearly.

Not everyone is prepared for this connection. The energy of dragons demands responsibility, as their influence can accelerate internal processes and bring to light aspects that need to be worked on. Many who seek this contact without being ready end up facing unexpected challenges, as the draconic presence exposes illusions and limiting patterns that need to be transformed. Those who wish to tread this path must be willing to face their own shadow and undergo a process of purification and spiritual strengthening.

The study of dragons in esotericism and spirituality is not limited to beliefs or dogmas. It represents a calling for those who feel a deep affinity with these beings and wish to understand their role in human evolution. Draconic energy does not belong to a single tradition but manifests in various ways, always guiding those who seek the truth beyond appearances.

For those who feel the presence of dragons and wish to deepen this connection, the path is open. It requires patience, respect, and a willingness to learn from these ancestral entities. Dragons are demanding masters, but they are also powerful allies for those who truly understand their essence and accept the journey they offer.

Chapter 4
Why Did They Leave?

The relationship between dragons and humanity has always been shrouded in mystery, woven into myths and traditions that span the ages. For eras, these beings were considered guardians of knowledge, spiritual allies, and cosmic forces that operated both in the material world and the subtle realms of existence. Yet, at some point in history, accounts of encounters with dragons became rare, their presence ceased to be recorded, and humanity began to treat them as mere figures of legend. What could have happened to cause these beings to seemingly vanish? This question resonates within various esoteric currents, which seek answers not only in history, but also in the spiritual planes and the hidden laws that govern reality.

One of the most widespread explanations within mystical traditions suggests that dragons never truly left, but simply concealed themselves in higher dimensions or vibrational states beyond ordinary perception. According to this view, their withdrawal from the visible world is directly linked to the decline of humanity's spiritual consciousness. In ancient times, advanced civilizations like Atlantis and Lemuria are said to have maintained direct contact with dragons, using their knowledge to expand their understanding of the universe and develop extraordinary abilities. However, as these societies began to abuse this power, ignoring the principles of balance and respect that sustained this relationship, the dragons reportedly withdrew, protecting themselves from human corruption and preventing their wisdom from being misused.

Another theory suggests that the dragons' departure was not voluntary, but rather imposed by forces that feared their influence. Some traditions speak of a time of great spiritual conflicts, in which powerful beings sought to subjugate or imprison the dragons, sealing their energy in hidden places or reducing their presence to a latent state. These stories mention the existence of portals and energy vortices where the draconic essence remains dormant, awaiting the opportune moment to reawaken. Some cultures interpret mountains, sacred caves, and even certain rock formations as petrified remnants of these beings, suggesting that their presence can still be felt by those with sufficient energetic sensitivity to perceive them.

Whatever the explanation, the dragons' withdrawal from human reality represented more than a simple disappearance – it marked a profound shift in the connection between humanity and the primordial forces of the universe. Some esoteric currents assert that dragons never left, but simply retreated from the visible plane, hiding in higher dimensions or vibrational states that most humans cannot perceive. According to this view, humanity lost the ability to interact with dragons because its own vibration became dense and disconnected from the subtle energies that govern the spiritual planes. As the collective consciousness moved away from natural and sacred principles, the dragons retreated to protect their own existence and prevent the misuse of their power.

Many mystical accounts suggest that there was a time when humans and dragons coexisted harmoniously. Ancient civilizations, such as the Lemurians and Atlanteans, are said to have maintained a direct connection with these beings, using their wisdom to expand their understanding of the universe and develop advanced spiritual technologies. However, when these civilizations began to collapse due to the abuse of knowledge and energy, the dragons are believed to have gradually withdrawn, leaving only traces of their presence in myths and legends.

Another esoteric theory suggests that dragons did not merely depart, but were sealed or imprisoned by forces that feared their power. There are accounts that indicate the existence of portals or specific locations where draconic energy remains dormant, awaiting the right moment to awaken. Some traditions speak of petrified dragons, whose bodies have become mountains, islands, or rock formations that still carry their ancestral vibration. Places like the Dragon Wall in China or certain mountain ranges around the world are cited as possible remnants of these dormant entities.

The disappearance of dragons can also be understood from a symbolic perspective. In various spiritual traditions, dragons represent cosmic forces of great intensity, often linked to the awakening of consciousness and personal transformation. The withdrawal of these energies may indicate a period in humanity's history when the focus shifted to materialism, the fragmentation of knowledge, and disconnection from subtle realities. The retreat of the dragons would therefore be a metaphor for the loss of ancestral wisdom and the ability to access higher dimensions of existence.

Some esoteric schools claim that dragons have not gone definitively, but remain accessible to those who dedicate themselves to finding them again. For these scholars, dragons continue to act as spiritual guides and guardians of occult knowledge, but only reveal themselves to those who demonstrate respect and preparation. Contemporary accounts of mystical experiences suggest that individuals initiated into certain practices can establish contact with dragons through dreams, astral projections, deep meditations, and specific rituals.

The disappearance of dragons may be linked to the vibrational decline of humanity. Many spiritual traditions maintain that the Earth has already gone through cycles of high energetic frequency, where human beings had a greater connection with the spiritual realms and elemental forces. As societies advanced in material terms, but became spiritually disconnected, the planet's frequency decreased, hindering contact with entities such as dragons. This would explain why, in ancient times, dragons were such present figures and, over the centuries, became mere myths.

The return of dragons has been mentioned in several modern spiritual channelings, indicating that these beings are gradually re-approaching humanity. This idea is aligned with the theory that the Earth is undergoing a new process of vibrational ascension, allowing previously lost spiritual connections to be re-established. Many spiritualists believe that dragons are waiting for humanity to regain its elevated consciousness so that they can once again interact directly with those who are prepared.

The Tibetan tradition preserves an interesting view of dragons, associating them with storm clouds and climate change. The lamas claim that dragons never disappeared, but continue to influence natural events and manifest themselves in moments of great transformation. According to this perspective, draconic energy can be felt in the Earth's cycles of renewal, in abrupt shifts in consciousness, and in the revelations that arise during periods of global transition.

The study of dragons within esotericism and spirituality reveals that these entities are much more than mythical figures. They represent ancestral forces that shape reality and that, at certain moments in history, were closer to humanity. Their apparent disappearance can be understood as a necessary withdrawal, a phase of silence before a new cycle of awakening. For those who wish to rediscover the dragons, the path lies not in external search, but in reconnecting with inner wisdom and elevating one's own spiritual vibration.

If the dragons truly departed, there are indications that their return is near. The growing interest in spirituality, the energy of the elements, and reconnection with the sacred may be a sign that humanity is preparing for this reunion. The call of the dragons never ceased completely. It simply waited for the right moment to be heard again.

Chapter 5
The Return of the Dragons

The prophecy of the dragons' return isn't just a myth lost in the pages of time; it's a call resonating deep within humanity's collective consciousness. Since ancient civilizations, there have been tales of these majestic beings, suggesting they never truly vanished, but merely retreated to subtle realms, awaiting the right moment to reappear. Their return, according to various spiritual and esoteric traditions, is directly linked to planetary transformation, the elevation of human consciousness, and the restoration of Earth's energetic balance. Dragons represent primordial forces that operate behind the scenes of existence, and their awakening would reflect humanity's need to reconnect with ancestral wisdom and the natural laws that govern the universe.

Different cultures preserve narratives pointing to this draconic rebirth. Some esoteric lineages claim that dragons have been in a state of dormancy, protecting themselves from humanity's spiritual degradation. Others believe their energy never ceased to act, but only the truly prepared can perceive them. Modern accounts of spiritual experiences indicate that many people have felt the presence of dragons in dreams, meditations, and mystical practices, as if their energy is becoming accessible again. These encounters are not mere coincidences, but signs that humanity is regaining its ability to tune into subtle forces that were beyond its perception.

The return of the dragons shouldn't be interpreted as a physical event, with winged creatures appearing in the skies, but rather as a reactivation of their energy and influence on Earth. Their awakening symbolizes a moment of transition, where ancient knowledge is reclaimed and new spiritual possibilities open up for those seeking truth. Those who feel this intuitive call are invited to deepen their connection with these beings, respecting their wisdom and understanding that their presence is a reminder of the inner power that each individual carries. The draconic awakening is both an internal process and a collective phenomenon, marking the beginning of a new era where balance between humanity, nature, and the cosmos can be restored.

Ancient texts and occult writings mention that the dragons' withdrawal wasn't an abandonment, but rather an act of protection. Some spiritual lineages maintain that the dragons, perceiving the degradation of human consciousness and the departure from natural laws, decided to hide themselves to prevent their knowledge from being corrupted or used for selfish purposes. They couldn't allow their power to be exploited by those who sought domination instead of wisdom. Thus, they retreated to other dimensions or reduced their vibration to a state where only the truly prepared could find them.

The prophecies that speak of the dragons' return are often associated with periods of great planetary transformation. Some spiritual traditions indicate that this return is directly linked to Earth's ascension to a new vibrational frequency. With humanity awakening to a higher consciousness, becoming more receptive to subtle realities, the dragons could be manifesting again to assist in this transition process. This concept is frequently related to the energetic shifts that have been felt worldwide, manifested in the increase of spiritual sensitivity, the search for reconnection with nature, and the growing interest in ancestral knowledge.

Some mystical visions suggest that dragons have always been close, but dormant in specific locations on the planet, awaiting the appropriate moment to awaken. Sacred places, where the Earth's energy is more intense, are frequently associated with draconic presence. There are reports that certain mountains, caves, and islands have direct connections with these entities, being activation points for those who know how to access them. Ley lines, which are flows of energy that run across the planet, are also mentioned as paths through which the dragons' power can return to the surface.

In the Chinese tradition, dragons are linked to the balance of natural forces. When there is disharmony in the world, it is said that dragons retreat to the heavens or dive into the depths of the earth and oceans, waiting for order to be restored. Some interpretations suggest that the return of the dragons will not be visible in the physical sense, but rather a reactivation of their energy, influencing the course of human events and awakening those who have an affinity with their vibration.

Many spiritualists report that the presence of dragons can be felt again through dreams, meditations, and experiences of expanded consciousness. There are accounts of people who had never thought of these beings, but suddenly began to receive visions or intuitions linked to dragons. Some describe encounters on astral planes, where they receive teachings or instructions to prepare humanity for a new cycle of existence. These reports are not isolated, and many esoteric cultures interpret them as signs that the dragons are gradually returning.

The relationship between dragons and planetary transformation can also be observed in the impact of the changes that have been occurring on Earth. Extreme weather events, energetic shifts, and global crises are seen by some spiritual lineages as part of the awakening process, and the dragons would be acting behind the scenes to stabilize these transitions. In some shamanic traditions, it is believed that dragons have direct influence over the elements of nature and that their return coincides with moments when the natural balance needs to be restored.

The idea that dragons are returning also manifests symbolically in the increased interest in their symbolism. More and more people seek to understand their essence, feeling an intuitive connection with these beings, even without fully understanding the reason. This phenomenon can be interpreted as an inner call, a gradual awakening of consciousness to realities that were dormant.

Those who believe in the prophecy of the dragons' return see this moment as an opportunity to recover forgotten wisdom. The knowledge that dragons hold is not only about the cosmos or the mysteries of existence, but also about the human essence itself. They teach about balance, courage, transformation, and connection with the forces that govern the universe. Their return should not be seen as an external event, but as an internal process, where humanity needs to become worthy of accessing this wisdom again.

The return of the dragons is not just an ancient legend or a symbolic myth. For those who feel their presence, it is a reminder that humanity's spiritual journey is entering a new stage. The draconic awakening will not happen for everyone, but only for those who seek this connection with honesty and respect. Draconic energy cannot be forced or manipulated, but it can be received by those who demonstrate that they are ready to walk the path of wisdom.

The prophecy of the dragons' return is not a future event, but something that is already underway. Their presence can be felt by those who are attentive to the signs, whether they are dreams, subtle encounters, or an inner call to seek knowledge long forgotten. The reunion between humans and dragons represents not only the restoration of an ancient bond, but also the ascension to a new understanding of existence and the role of humanity in the cosmic balance.

Chapter 6
The Dragons and the Four Elements

Dragons are ancestral entities deeply intertwined with the primordial forces of the universe, acting as guardians and catalysts of the fundamental energies that sustain all existence. More than mythical creatures, they represent the conscious manifestation of the four elements – fire, water, earth, and air – holding wisdom and power. Their presence is felt in all spiritual and philosophical traditions that seek to understand the energetic structure of the cosmos. Each dragon resonates with a specific element, channeling its forces and balancing the natural dynamics that govern reality. This connection is not limited to mythology; it reflects a hidden truth about the interconnectedness between living beings and the energy flows that permeate creation. Since time immemorial, dragons have been revered as bridges between the material and subtle planes, guiding those who wish to delve into the harmony of the elements and access the hidden mysteries of existence.

The interaction between dragons and the elements is not merely symbolic, but rather a vibrational relationship that shapes how these forces express themselves in the world. Fire represents the flame of transformation and indomitable will, the impulse of creation and constant renewal. Water symbolizes emotional fluidity and intuitive wisdom, the reflection of the unconscious and the depths of the soul. Earth embodies stability, the foundation of materialization and protection, while air carries the freedom of thought, mental clarity, and connection to higher dimensions. Dragons, as interdimensional entities, act as transmitters of these energies, serving as a link between humanity and the essential elements of life. Those who learn to recognize and respect this connection find a path of self-knowledge and expansion, for the elements are not only external but also manifest within each individual, reflecting inner aspects of the psyche and spirit.

The quest for balance between the four elements is, in truth, an invitation to integrate the self with the universe. Dragons teach that there is no supremacy among these forces, as all are indispensable for the harmony of existence. Those who wish to understand their essence must allow themselves to feel the presence of these energies in their daily lives – in the flame that warms and purifies, in the water that nourishes and heals, in the earth that sustains and strengthens, in the air that inspires and connects. By recognizing the influence of dragons on these aspects, it becomes possible to access a deeper level of perception and attunement with nature and oneself. Elemental dragons, far from being mere myths, are living entities in the subtle realms, always ready to share their wisdom with those who show themselves ready to learn.

The connection of dragons with the elements is not only symbolic, but energetic. They vibrate in tune with these forces and act as intermediaries between the physical plane and the subtle realms. By understanding how dragons interact with each element, it becomes possible to access their energies more consciously, allowing a deep connection with nature and one's own inner power.

Fire dragons represent the transformative energy of creation and destruction. They are symbols of vital impulse, willpower, and the awakening of consciousness. Their presence is intense and ignites everything that is not aligned with truth, burning away illusions and strengthening those who seek evolution. The energy of fire dragons is associated with transmutation, rebirth, and the courage needed to overcome challenges and fears. Working with this energy requires balance, as fire can both illuminate and consume.

Water dragons symbolize the fluidity of emotions and the depth of intuition. They are the guardians of feelings, the unconscious, and the mysteries that reside in the hidden waters of the soul. They assist in emotional healing, expanding sensitivity, and connecting with ancestral memories. Just as water can be gentle and serene or violent and destructive, these dragons teach how to deal with the flows of life, accepting changes and learning to navigate challenges with wisdom.

Earth dragons are the pillars of stability and protection. They represent the power of materialization, the connection with roots, and the support of energetic structures. Their presence brings security and alignment, helping to build solid foundations for any spiritual journey. They are associated with patience, resilience, and the ancestral wisdom that manifests through the earth and its cycles. The energy of these dragons aids in strengthening the body, physical healing, and alignment with the vital force of nature.

Air dragons are messengers of cosmic wisdom, responsible for expanding the mind and interdimensional communication. They represent clarity of thought, inspiration, and the ability to transcend limitations. Working with their energy allows one to access new perspectives, understand hidden truths, and develop sharper intuitive abilities. Air dragons are also responsible for opening paths to connect with higher planes, facilitating communication with spiritual beings and allowing a more harmonious flow of ideas and insights.

The relationship between dragons and the elements is not fixed, as they can transition between these energies as needed. Some carry mixed characteristics, uniting the power of fire with the fluidity of water or the solidity of earth with the lightness of air. These hybrid dragons are rarer and are usually invoked in specific situations, when the integration of multiple aspects of reality is necessary.

Connection with elemental dragons can be established through observation and respect for natural forces. Each person carries within them the manifestation of these four elements, and by balancing them, they become more receptive to the presence of dragons. Working with the elements is a way to better understand one's own essence, developing a more conscious relationship with the world around.

Dragons not only govern the elements, but also teach how to use them in a balanced way. Those who seek draconic wisdom learn that there is no element superior to another, as all are parts of a single energy flow. Fire can give life or consume, water can heal or drown, earth can sustain or imprison, and air can bring clarity or confusion. True mastery lies in knowing how to work with each energy at the right time.

Dragons and the elements are deeply connected to spiritual awakening. Many spiritual traditions use the elements as a basis for their practices, whether in shamanism, alchemy, or ceremonial magic. Dragons appear in these traditions as guardians of energetic portals, assisting those who seek to understand and manipulate these forces with wisdom and respect.

The presence of elemental dragons can be perceived in nature, in intense climatic phenomena, in places of great energetic power, or even in personal experiences of transformation. When a person connects deeply with an element, whether through a moment of introspection by the sea, the heat of a flame, contact with the earth, or the sensation of the wind, there is a chance that they are feeling the presence of a corresponding dragon, manifesting subtly to convey a lesson or a message.

Those who wish to establish a deeper contact with elemental dragons can use practices such as meditation, creative visualization, and direct connection with the elements of nature. Creating an environment conducive to this interaction, respecting natural cycles and opening oneself to the experience, can facilitate the perception of these subtle forces.

Dragons and the elements are inseparable parts of existence, reflecting both the forces of the universe and the inner aspects of each individual. Understanding this connection is an important step to accessing draconic wisdom and developing a more balanced relationship with the energies that sustain reality. As humanity awakens to this understanding, dragons begin to manifest again, guiding those who are ready to receive their teaching and protection.

Chapter 7
Dragons of Fire

The energy of fire dragons pulses with a primal force that challenges and transforms everything it touches. These draconic entities aren't merely symbols of burning flame; they are living manifestations of the sacred fire that permeates existence. They represent the principle of creation and destruction, the energy that drives evolution, challenging stagnation and rekindling the will to grow. Their presence is felt in moments of great transition, when old patterns must be burned away to make way for the new. They are guardians of spiritual awakening, bringing the light of consciousness to illuminate what was hidden and to dissolve illusions. The fire of these dragons is neither docile nor complacent; it demands courage from those who invoke it, for its action is intense and irreversible. Those who connect with this energy are called to abandon limitations, break down barriers, and become active agents of their own transformation.

Fire dragons vibrate with the frequency of courage and inner strength. Their energy awakens the flame of determination, propelling those who hesitate before the unknown. They are masters of transmutation, aiding in overcoming fears, freeing emotional bonds, and strengthening the spirit. Unlike other protective forces that offer gentle support, fire dragons teach through confrontation and direct experience. They don't remove obstacles, but empower those who face them. Their purpose isn't to offer an easy path, but rather to strengthen those who walk the journey of self-discovery and empowerment. When working with this energy, it's crucial to understand that fire can both illuminate and warm, as well as consume and destroy. It demands respect and mastery, because its intensity, if uncontrolled, can lead to impulsiveness and chaos.

Those who feel the call of fire dragons must be willing to embrace change without fear. Their presence marks the beginning of a cycle of profound transformation, where everything that doesn't resonate with inner truth will be consumed by the flames. This process, though challenging, leads to rebirth, the expansion of consciousness, and the awakening of true potential. Connecting with a fire dragon means accepting that the journey will be intense, but also liberating. Their flame doesn't destroy out of cruelty, but to make space for something stronger and more authentic. By accepting this energy and learning to channel it wisely, it becomes possible to access an unshakeable inner power, capable of shaping reality with clarity, passion, and purpose.

Fire is associated with vital energy, the creative impulse, and renewal. Just as a flame can consume what no longer serves and allow something new to be born, fire dragons assist in the process of inner transmutation. They teach us to burn away limitations, dissolve fears, and expand our inner strength. They are guardians of courage, dynamism, and iron will, encouraging those who connect with their energy to overcome obstacles and challenges with determination.

The presence of a fire dragon can be felt during times of great change and crisis, when life demands transformation and renewal. Their energy is intense and often uncomfortable, as it doesn't allow for stagnation. Where there is resistance to change, the fire burns, forcing a complete restructuring. This process can manifest in various areas of life, from personal relationships to professional changes and spiritual challenges.

In the spiritual realm, fire dragons are linked to the awakening of consciousness. Their inner flame illuminates hidden truths and dissolves illusions, allowing for a clearer vision of the path ahead. They activate the power of the solar plexus chakra, where the energy of will, self-confidence, and the ability to act resides. Working with this energy strengthens determination and the capacity to manifest intentions in the material world.

The energy of fire dragons is also deeply connected to purification. They consume dense energies and emotional blockages, allowing the vital flow to return to its natural state. This process can be challenging, as it requires old patterns and limiting beliefs to be confronted and eliminated. Many people report intense experiences when working with this force, feeling body heat, impulses to act, and an awakening of instinctive intuition.

Fire dragons are powerful allies for those who wish to break with the past and begin a new phase of life. They teach the importance of detachment, as fire cannot be contained or imprisoned. To follow their path, one must trust the process and allow the transformation to occur. When this energy is accepted, it brings renewal and empowerment, allowing the individual to take control of their own journey.

Many spiritual traditions relate fire dragons to the archetype of the spiritual warrior, the one who faces their shadows and challenges with bravery. They are not complacent or protective in the traditional sense, as their purpose is not to avoid difficulties, but rather to strengthen those who face them. Their main teaching is self-sufficiency and the discovery of one's own inner power.

Connection with fire dragons can be established through meditation practices, visualizations, and direct contact with the element of fire. Lighting candles or bonfires and meditating before the flames can be a powerful way to access this energy. Specific mantras and invocations can also be used to call their presence and ask for guidance. However, this energy should not be sought irresponsibly, as its intensity can be overwhelming for those who are not prepared.

Fire dragons also teach about balance. Although their energy is transformative, excess can lead to destruction and lack of control. Just as fire needs boundaries to be useful, inner strength must be channeled wisely to avoid becoming impulsiveness or aggression. One who learns to master this inner flame becomes a master of their own energy, capable of acting with determination without being consumed by excessive power.

The call of fire dragons resonates with those who are ready to change and evolve. Their presence marks the beginning of a journey of empowerment and transformation, where everything that is not true will be consumed by the flames. Those who accept this energy learn that fire does not destroy out of cruelty, but to make way for something new and more aligned with their true essence. The path of transmutation is intense, but it leads to rebirth and the awakening of true inner strength.

Chapter 8
Water Dragons

Water dragons emerge from the depths of the unconscious as guardians of emotional flow and ancestral knowledge. Unlike the impetuous and transformative forces of fire, these dragons act subtly, shaping emotions and guiding individuals through life's natural cycles. They are the personification of fluidity, teaching that adaptation and acceptance are paths to inner harmony and growth. Their domain extends to oceans, rivers, and rains, reflecting water's ability to nurture, purify, and transform. Connection with these beings invites introspection, encouraging those who seek their wisdom to dive deep within themselves to understand the hidden layers of their emotions, fears, and dreams. Their call is not thunderous, but rather a whisper in the tides of the soul, gently guiding towards clarity and balance.

Water has the power to carve mountains, to break through barriers with persistence, and to reflect truth with crystalline purity. Similarly, the dragons that carry this essence teach the importance of patience and trust in the natural processes of existence. They are masters of detachment and surrender, demonstrating that resistance only amplifies suffering, while acceptance paves the way for genuine transformation. By interacting with their energies, it becomes possible to access ancestral memories and reveal hidden truths that lay dormant in the depths of the mind. They are protectors of the unconscious and the mysteries that hide beneath the surface of reality, conveying messages through dreams, visions, and sudden intuitions. For those who tune into their vibration, water dragons offer silent guidance, helping to navigate life's challenges with serenity and understanding.

The presence of these dragons can be felt during moments of great emotional transition, when repressed feelings surface or when the soul yearns for clarity and healing. Their energy does not impose, but invites self-knowledge, allowing each individual to discover their own truth through contemplation and the natural flow of life. Working with the energy of water dragons requires openness to feeling, intuition, and the subtle signs of the universe. Those who learn from them develop a deep connection with their own essence, becoming more receptive to the wisdom of the heart and the cycles that govern existence. Just as water shapes the earth, the teachings of these dragons transform the perception of reality, showing that true strength lies not in rigidity, but in the ability to adapt and flow with confidence.

Water has the power to adapt to any form, to bypass obstacles, and to sculpt mountains over time. So too are the dragons that belong to this element. They teach the importance of flexibility and acceptance, showing that resistance often causes unnecessary suffering. Their energy allows repressed emotions to be brought to the surface and processed in a healthy way, helping to dissolve emotional blockages that hinder spiritual and personal growth.

Water dragons are especially connected to the world of dreams and visions. Many people report encounters with these beings in altered states of consciousness, where they manifest in undulating and luminous forms, bringing messages that seem to emerge from the depths of the subconscious. Unlike fire dragons, which challenge and propel, water dragons whisper gentle truths, encouraging introspection and inner listening.

The energy of water is connected to emotions and the fluidity of feelings. When a person feels trapped in destructive emotional patterns or past hurts, water dragons assist in the healing process, dissolving tensions and bringing clarity. Their presence can be felt in moments of deep introspection, when there is a need to understand one's own emotions and release what no longer serves.

Just as the oceans hide unfathomable mysteries, water dragons also guard knowledge forgotten by humanity. Some esoteric traditions claim that these beings maintain records of lost civilizations and ancestral secrets, stored in the planet's energy currents. Those who manage to access their wisdom are able to understand hidden patterns of history and access information that transcends time and space.

Water dragons also teach about the power of surrender and trust. Unlike the active energy of fire dragons, which demand action and determination, water dragons teach the importance of flowing with the events of life, without resistance or fear. This does not mean passivity, but rather a wise acceptance of the natural cycles of existence. When one learns to flow, life becomes more harmonious, and challenges are faced with serenity.

Connection with these dragons can be strengthened through contact with water in its various forms. Baths in rivers, seas, or waterfalls, as well as meditative practices near water, can facilitate this interaction. Visualizing a water dragon during meditation can open channels of communication with its energy, allowing intuitive messages to emerge more clearly.

Water dragons are also linked to the heart chakra and the sacral chakra, places where emotions and creative energy flow. Working with this energy helps to open the heart to unconditional love and to develop a sharper intuition. People who have an affinity with these dragons are generally sensitive, empathetic, and have a strong connection to the emotional and psychic world.

Those who tune into water dragons learn that true strength lies not in rigidity, but in the ability to adapt. Water does not resist, but bypasses. It does not fight, but transforms. Its wisdom lies in the ability to flow and find its way, regardless of the obstacles that arise. By understanding this lesson, it becomes possible to navigate life with more lightness and balance, trusting that everything is following the right course.

Water dragons are always present, guiding those who allow themselves to dive into their own depth.

Their energy calms, heals, and awakens. For those seeking wisdom and understanding, they reveal hidden truths and bring insights that can completely transform the way one perceives reality. Working with these dragons is learning to trust one's own intuition and to connect with the fluidity of existence.

Chapter 9
Earth Dragons

Earth dragons embody solidity, resilience, and a deep connection to the primordial forces that sustain existence. They are guardians of natural cycles and keepers of ancestral wisdom, teaching that true strength lies not in haste or impulsiveness, but in the patient and careful construction of the foundations that support life. Their energy is dense and stabilizing, providing security to those who seek balance and structure. Unlike the mutable forces of fire and water, which represent transformation and fluidity, earth dragons teach the value of constancy, discipline, and permanence. They represent the very essence of matter, reminding us that everything that grows and thrives needs fertile and firm soil. Their lessons are conveyed through patience and respect for time, showing that any true development must be rooted in solid foundations to endure.

Just as mountains are formed over millennia, earth dragons teach that all construction requires dedication and perseverance. Their presence is felt in places where the earth's energy manifests intensely—caves, ancient forests, imposing rock formations, and untouched lands. They are protectors of the planet's memory, guarding forgotten secrets and knowledge hidden deep within the soil. Many spiritual accounts indicate that connecting with these dragons awakens a sense of belonging and alignment with natural laws. Unlike celestial forces that expand consciousness beyond the material plane, earth dragons help to anchor energy, ensuring that spiritual expansion occurs with balance and stability. They are powerful allies for those who wish to transform abstract ideas into something concrete, materializing aspirations in a structured and conscious way.

Working with the energy of earth dragons means understanding that haste often weakens the foundation upon which life is built. They teach us to respect the time needed for each process, reminding us that everything has its own rhythm of growth. Connection with these dragons can be strengthened through immersion in nature, direct contact with the earth, and observation of natural cycles. Meditations that involve visualizing deep roots, strengthening the connection with the earthly essence, help to tune into their stabilizing energy. Those who learn from earth dragons discover that true power lies not only in the ability to advance, but in the ability to sustain, protect, and preserve. When this lesson is understood, it becomes possible to build a life grounded in security, solidity, and harmony with the primordial forces of the universe.

The earth is the foundation upon which all life develops. It provides food, shelter, and support, ensuring that everything has a solid base to grow from. Similarly, earth dragons teach the importance of patience, perseverance, and respect for natural cycles. Their presence reminds us that nothing is built without foundations and that haste often leads to instability. Working with this energy means understanding that everything has its time and that true growth occurs gradually and consistently.

Many ancient traditions associate earth dragons with mountains, caves, and forests. These places, considered sacred, are seen as portals where the earth's energy manifests most intensely. There are accounts of meditations and spiritual experiences in which people have felt the presence of these dragons in remote locations, as if they were protecting ancestral secrets hidden deep within the earth.

These dragons are also considered guardians of hidden treasures. Unlike what popular legends suggest, these treasures are not just material riches, but ancient knowledge, stored in protected places for those who demonstrate the maturity to access them. The metaphor of the dragon sleeping on a pile of gold symbolizes the ancestral wisdom that awaits discovery by those who truly understand its value.

The energy of earth dragons is one of protection and resilience. They help create energetic barriers against negative influences and strengthen the auric field of those seeking security and balance. Many people who work with spirituality report that connecting with these dragons provides a sense of solidity and security, as if they were being enveloped by a force that keeps everything in order and aligned.

In the human body, this energy is associated with the root chakra, located at the base of the spine. This chakra governs the sense of security, connection to physical reality, and emotional stability. When this energy center is strong, a person feels firm in their journey, confident, and resistant to external challenges. Earth dragons assist in activating this chakra, helping to build a solid foundation for any type of growth, be it material, emotional, or spiritual.

Those who connect with earth dragons learn the importance of respecting natural laws. Unlike air dragons, which seek expansion, or fire dragons, which drive transformation, earth dragons teach the art of patience and constancy. Everything in nature follows a rhythm, and trying to accelerate processes can lead to imbalance. This lesson is reflected in everyday life, where learning to wait for the right time for everything brings much more solid and lasting results.

The relationship with the energy of earth dragons can be strengthened through direct contact with nature. Walking barefoot, touching trees, feeling the texture of the earth in your hands are simple but powerful ways to reconnect with this energy. Meditations focused on visualizing roots that deepen into the soil, connecting to the primordial energy of the Earth, are also effective in strengthening this connection.

Earth dragons are great allies for those who wish to build something lasting in their lives. Whether it's projects, relationships, or a spiritual path, they teach that everything of value must be cultivated with patience and dedication. Their presence inspires security and confidence, ensuring that the foundations are strong enough to withstand any challenge.

The energy of these dragons reminds us that there is no true growth without a foundation. Before expanding, one must take root. Before advancing, one must strengthen. And before reaching great heights, it is necessary to have a solid base to lean on. Working with earth dragons is to accept this principle and understand that, in due time, everything blossoms and manifests in the most balanced and harmonious way possible.

Chapter 10
Dragons of Air

Air dragons embody the essence of freedom, wisdom, and the expansion of consciousness, acting as subtle forces that transcend the limitations of the material world. They represent sharp intellect, heightened intuition, and a connection to higher planes of existence. Unlike earth dragons, who ground and stabilize, or fire dragons, who propel and transform with intensity, air dragons serve as messengers of cosmic knowledge, carrying the lightness of the wind and the depth of thoughts that move beyond time and space. They are masters of communication, inspiring ideas, insights, and understandings that often seem to arise from nowhere, but are, in truth, whispers of wisdom breathed by these ethereal beings. Their presence is felt as a call to seek understanding, broaden perspectives, and break free from the shackles of limited thinking.

Air is an invisible yet indispensable element for life, and so too are the dragons that belong to it. They manifest through sudden intuition, innovative ideas, and the mental clarity that emerges like a ray of light amidst the darkness of doubt. They are guardians of ancestral and interdimensional knowledge, connecting those who seek them to the vastness of the universe and its infinite possibilities. In many spiritual traditions, they are seen as beings who aid in communication with higher planes, helping to understand messages that cannot be grasped by the physical senses alone. Their energy resonates in the breath of the wind, the flight of birds, the movement of clouds, and the silence pregnant with meaning that precedes a great revelation. Connection with these dragons occurs in the space between thoughts, where the mind quiets enough to perceive the truths that have always been there, waiting to be discovered.

Working with the energy of air dragons is an invitation to expansion and to intellectual and spiritual transformation. They teach that rigidity of thought limits evolution, and that true wisdom lies in flexibility and the ability to see beyond appearances. They inspire creativity, curiosity, and the will to explore new paths, helping those who connect with their essence to dissolve limiting beliefs and accept that knowledge is never static, but rather a continuous flow of discoveries. To establish this connection, it is essential to cultivate silence, contemplation, and observation of nature, allowing the mind to become an open sky, ready to receive the messages that the wind carries. Those who attune themselves to air dragons learn to trust their intuition, perceive subtle signs around them, and embrace the freedom of thought, understanding that the journey of learning never ends, but is an eternal flight towards a deeper understanding of the universe and oneself.

The element of air is invisible, yet essential. It is present at all times, filling the space around us and sustaining life with every breath. Just as the wind carries seeds to distant lands, air dragons disseminate ideas, connect dimensions, and inspire those who are ready to listen. They are known for their ability to bring messages from the universe, manifesting through sudden insights, accurate intuitions, and a sense of mental clarity that may seem to come out of nowhere.

Ancient cultures often associated air dragons with beings that mastered the skies and served as intermediaries between worlds. In many mythologies, gods and higher spirits traveled on winged dragons, symbolizing their ability to transcend the limits of the physical world. In shamanic traditions, the wind and air currents were seen as channels of communication between spirits and humans, and air dragons were considered guides capable of transmitting sacred knowledge to those who could attune to their frequency.

Those who seek connection with air dragons are usually individuals who feel a calling to expand their consciousness and access higher levels of understanding. These dragons work with intellect and perception, helping to develop intuition and spiritual communication. When an air dragon approaches, it is common for its presence to be perceived as a lightness in the environment, a breath of inspiration, or even signs in nature, such as sudden changes in the wind.

The chakra associated with air dragons is the throat chakra, which governs communication and expression. Working with this energy strengthens the ability to express oneself clearly, whether verbally, artistically, or spiritually. Many people who develop this connection find it easier to translate their ideas into words, access new forms of knowledge, and communicate with other planes of existence.

Air dragons are also linked to the ability to travel between dimensions. Some esoteric traditions claim that they can open portals to higher realities, allowing those who connect with their energy to glimpse other existences and understand aspects of the universe that would normally be beyond the reach of the human mind. Their presence can be felt in deep meditative states, where the flow of thoughts becomes clearer and the mind seems to expand beyond its usual limits.

Connection with air dragons can be cultivated through practices that involve conscious breathing, outdoor meditation, and contemplation of the sky. Observing the moving clouds, feeling the breeze on your face, and paying attention to the rhythm of the wind are subtle, yet powerful, ways to tune into this energy. Some people report that, when asking these dragons for guidance, they receive unexpected answers through coincidences, words from strangers, or even messages that seem to arise spontaneously in their minds.

Air dragons also teach about the importance of lightness and adaptability. Just as the wind changes direction effortlessly, these dragons show that mental rigidity and resistance to change can be obstacles to evolution. Those who learn to flow with the energy of air discover that life becomes more harmonious when they allow themselves to change perspective and accept new possibilities.

However, just as a storm can arise suddenly, the energy of air dragons can also bring moments of turbulence. When their presence is strong, accelerated thoughts, intense insights, and a sense of restlessness may arise. This occurs because their vibration activates the mind, stimulating the search for answers and new directions. To balance this energy, it is important to maintain moments of pause and introspection, allowing ideas to organize themselves naturally.

Air dragons are great allies for those who wish to expand their horizons and understand the interconnectedness of all things. They help to dissolve illusions, perceive hidden patterns, and access knowledge that was beyond the reach of the conscious mind. Often, their presence marks the beginning of a period of spiritual awakening, where the perception of reality expands and new truths begin to emerge.

Those who connect with air dragons learn that wisdom is not only found in books or words, but also in the spaces between them. Silence, the wind, and the movement of clouds carry messages for those who know how to listen. Working with this energy is opening oneself to the unknown, allowing the flow of the universe to bring the right answers at the right time.

The journey with air dragons is an invitation to elevate the mind, expand consciousness, and trust in the wisdom that circulates through the cosmos. Their main teaching is that true knowledge is not found in the rigidity of certainties, but in the freedom to explore, question, and discover. Those who accept this call learn to fly beyond the limitations of the mind and see the world with new eyes, becoming travelers of the infinite wisdom that air dragons carry with them.

Chapter 11
The Spiritual Awakening and the Dragons

The presence of dragons on the path of spiritual awakening reveals a profound connection between these entities and the human journey of self-discovery. Since time immemorial, dragons have been depicted as guardians of hidden knowledge, bearers of ancestral secrets that only the prepared can access. Different cultures around the world describe them as beings of immense power, symbols of transformation and mastery over natural forces. Their energy resonates not only with aspects of creation and destruction, but also with spiritual ascension, guiding those who are on a quest for a deeper understanding of existence.

In the context of the awakening of consciousness, dragons act as powerful allies, guiding the individual through a process of growth that demands courage, discipline, and a genuine openness to evolution. Their presence, whether through dreams, visions, or subtle intuitions, indicates that the soul is ready to cross a new portal of understanding, connecting to higher dimensions of reality.

The spiritual awakening, driven by the power of dragons, does not occur randomly or without purpose. It is, in fact, an inner calling, a response of the soul to the yearning for something greater than material reality. This process can begin with a feeling of restlessness, a sense that there is more to be understood beyond the physical world. Often, those who experience this transformation report symbolic encounters with dragons in moments of deep introspection, as if these entities were waiting for the right moment to manifest.

These encounters are not mere coincidences, but reflections of a connection that strengthens as the individual expands their perception. Dragons, in these cases, act as catalysts, accelerating internal changes and promoting a broader view of existence. They help dissolve energetic blockages, strengthen intuition, and awaken latent abilities that remained dormant. Thus, interaction with these spiritual forces is not simply a mystical event, but a transformative experience that reconfigures the way one perceives one's own journey.

This link between dragons and spiritual awakening is also manifested in the way these beings challenge and test those who seek their wisdom. Unlike spiritual guides who offer ready-made answers or safe paths, dragons encourage individuals to face their fears, overcome self-imposed limitations, and recognize their true potential. They demand commitment and respect, as they do not share their knowledge with those who do not demonstrate the maturity to receive it.

In many esoteric traditions, the dragon represents the union of opposites – light and shadow, creation and destruction, fear and courage. This symbolism reflects the very process of awakening, which involves confronting internal aspects that have been neglected or

The connection with dragons is not something that can be forced. It occurs when the individual is ready to receive their teachings. Some people may feel their presence since childhood, while others only establish this connection later, when they have already gone through internal processes that have prepared them for this experience. The important thing is that this contact is not random – it happens when there is a real purpose, whether for learning, protection, or spiritual evolution.

One of the most effective ways to deepen this connection is through meditation and visualization. Creating a space of tranquility and allowing oneself to enter a state of receptivity can facilitate contact with the draconic energy. During these practices, it is common for images or sensations to arise spontaneously, indicating the presence of these beings. Some people report that their dragons present themselves in specific ways, with unique colors and characteristics, each representing an aspect of their personal journey.

Another method of strengthening this connection is through observation of nature. Dragons are closely linked to the elements, and their energies can be felt in natural environments, such as forests, mountains, rivers, and deserts. Spending time in places where the earth's energy is purer can help tune into their frequency, making it easier to perceive their presence.

Dragons are not just spiritual symbols; they are living forces that interact with those who are prepared to receive them. Their energy is intense and can accelerate awakening processes that were dormant. However, they do not do this work alone. The person needs to be willing to look inside themselves, to face their shadows and to take responsibility for their own evolution.

Spiritual awakening influenced by dragons is not a path for everyone. It requires commitment, courage, and a genuine desire for transformation. Those who accept this call discover a new world, where the limits of reality expand and new possibilities open up. Dragons guide this process with strength and wisdom, showing that the spiritual journey is not a fixed destination, but a constant evolution.

The presence of dragons in human spirituality has always been linked to the search for true knowledge. In ancient times, only the initiated had access to their mysteries, and those who tried to approach without proper preparation often failed. Today, with the collective awakening of humanity, these teachings are becoming more accessible, and more and more people feel the call to rediscover this lost connection.

Spiritual awakening is a rebirth. It is the discovery that the world goes beyond what the physical eyes can see and that reality is much vaster and interconnected than one imagines. Dragons are part of this process, guiding those who are ready to understand their presence and receive their teachings. For those who feel this call, the journey has just begun. The dragons watch, wait, and, when the time is right, make themselves present to those who are prepared to fly alongside them.

Chapter 12
Energy Portals

The Earth's landscape is interwoven with a network of invisible forces, energy flows that course through its expanse like the pulsating arteries of a living organism. These energy channels, known by different names in various spiritual traditions, form a vibrant web connecting mountains, forests, oceans, and deserts in a dynamic and interconnected pattern. Certain points within this vast circuit radiate a unique intensity, functioning as energy portals, where the boundary between the tangible and the subtle becomes thin. These locations are more than mere geographical accidents; they represent points of convergence between telluric and cosmic forces, where the flow of energy intensifies, providing experiences of spiritual connection, healing, and expanded consciousness. Ancient civilizations, perceiving these emanations, erected monuments, temples, and astronomical alignments to mark and potentiate these spaces, recognizing them as centers of power and wisdom. The constant presence of myths and legends associated with these places reveals that, since time immemorial, humanity has felt the impact of these forces and sought to understand them.

Within this context, the link between energy portals and the forces of nature unfolds even more profoundly, manifesting in the symbolism of dragons. Far from being mere creatures of folklore, these entities are frequently described as guardians of the Earth's great energy flows. In many traditions, dragons represent the primordial force that winds through the planet, analogous to the energy lines that run through the ground and meet in these vortexes of power. Ancient cultures perceived this correspondence and associated dragons with the protection of sacred caves, ancestral rivers, imposing mountains, and places of intense spiritual charge. These stories did not arise by chance; they reflect an intuitive perception of the living nature of these portals and the presence of spiritual intelligences that watch over them and maintain their balance. Thus, interaction with an energy portal is not limited to a geographical or magnetic phenomenon, but involves contact with forces that transcend matter, opening doors to more subtle dimensions of reality.

The human experience with these portals varies according to the sensitivity and disposition of each individual. For those who approach with reverence and clear intention, these places can reveal themselves as points of profound transformation. Many report inexplicable sensations upon stepping on certain grounds: a tingling throughout the body, a change in the perception of time, vivid dreams, or even striking spiritual encounters. In certain cultures, pilgrims perform rituals to "ask permission" before entering these sacred spaces, recognizing the presence of the energy guardians – often symbolized by the dragons themselves. This act is not just a formality, but a recognition that these portals are not mere geographical anomalies, but points of contact between different levels of existence. Therefore, understanding and respecting energy portals also means understanding the ancient connection between the Earth, its vital flows, and the subtle consciousnesses that inhabit them.

In this context of telluric and subtle forces, dragons reveal themselves as an intrinsic part of this great planetary organism. Various cultures around the globe have portrayed dragons not only as mythical beings, but also as personifications of the energies of nature. It is common for millenary legends to place dragons in sacred mountains, thermal springs, deep caves, or ancient oaks – precisely places associated with the intensified flow of Earth's energy. This symbolic connection suggests that dragons are intimately linked to energy portals, acting as guardians and facilitators of these forces. In spiritual terms, we can understand them as ancestral intelligences that inhabit the subtle field of the planet, manifesting through these vortexes of power when certain conditions are met.

Around the world, there are traditions that link dragons to points of great power. In Asia, for example, there is the Chinese concept of "dragon lines" – the ancient masters of feng shui believed that currents of energy run through the earth in serpentine veins, and that where these lines intersect, places of singular force emerge. In these points, it is said that celestial dragons rest or watch. Mountains revered as Mount Kunlun and

Mount Song, in China, are considered homes of dragons and coincide with vital energy lines of the territory. In Japan, legends of the dragon god Ryūjin place his presence in deep lakes and crystal springs; not by chance, many of these places are considered portals between the human world and the spiritual realms. The cultures of the Himalayas also tell of dragons hidden in the peaks and sacred lagoons of Tibet, associated with unusual clouds and sudden winds in the silent heights – signs, the monks say, of the activity of invisible draconic forces.

In Europe, the correspondence between energy portals and draconic mythology is also evident. The Celts and other ancient peoples built monuments in peculiar places where the earth's energy seemed to vibrate more intensely. Stonehenge, in England, and other stone circles were erected on veins of force that we now call ley lines. Curiously, later oral traditions associate serpents or dragons with these sites, echoing the perception of a serpentine power there. In Welsh folklore, there is talk of dragons under the hills: the legend of Dinas Emrys tells of a red dragon and a white dragon sleeping inside the mountain and disputing the fate of the kingdom. The mountain associated with this legend coincides with a focus of telluric energy pointed out by modern geomancers. In Slavic lands, in Poland, Wawel Hill in Krakow is famous for the legend of the Wawel Dragon, who lived in a cave under the castle. Coincidentally (or not), this same place is revered by current mystics as housing an "Earth chakra", a source of subtle energy emanating from the ancient rocks.

Thus, we see a pattern: where there is a powerful energy portal, there is often a dragon in the stories of the people, as if the collective consciousness had perceived a guardian presence there.

In the Americas, from north to south, we also find this link between great serpents or dragons and places of power. In the Andes, Lake Titicaca and Machu Picchu stand out as revered energy centers. Myths speak of titanic serpents, like the Amaru, inhabiting the depths of Titicaca, while many visitors to Machu Picchu describe feeling an ancestral guardian winding through the mountains at dawn. In Mesoamerica, the Mayan civilization bequeathed us the pyramid of Kukulkan in Chichen Itza, dedicated to the feathered serpent god – a celestial dragon whose return is staged when the equinox light descends the staircase in the form of a serpent of shadows. This spectacle is not only astronomical, but also symbolic: it represents the opening of a portal between heaven and earth, a moment when the draconic deity touches the human world with its wisdom and strength.

But how can we, ordinary individuals, perceive and interact with these energy portals? The key is to sharpen our subtle senses and cultivate an attitude of respect and openness. Many of the planet's power points do not reveal their energy to an inattentive or skeptical observer. It is necessary to enter such places with the same reverence with which one enters a living temple of nature. By silencing the mind and calming the breath, we begin to feel the environment differently: a slight tingling throughout the body, or subtle changes in the temperature and density of the air around. Sometimes the feeling is emotional – a sudden peace or, on the contrary, an uneasiness that does not seem to come from us. These are indications that we are interacting with the local energy field. Visualization techniques can intensify this connection – for example, imagining roots of light sprouting from our feet and penetrating the ground, or visualizing ourselves enveloped by a spiral of ascending light connecting body and sky. Knowing the history and mythology of the place also helps: by mentally evoking the symbols of the dragon or the associated guardian, we synchronize our mind with the spiritual egregore of that portal.

Interacting with an energy portal requires sensitivity and humility. Shamans and mystics teach that we must "ask permission" from the guardians of the place – and here dragons play a central role as spiritual guardians. In practice, this means that upon arriving at one of these places, one makes a respectful prayer or intention, demonstrating goodwill and respect for the forces present there. One can, for example, touch the earth with the palm of the hand and mentalize a greeting to the spirit of the place. If there is indeed a draconic presence or other guardian consciousness, this attitude of reverence helps to open a channel of subtle communication. Some people report receiving "answers" intuitively: impressions, mental images, or a sudden clarity of thought, as if the place were telling them secrets in silence. Interacting is also knowing how to listen. Staying still, observing the nature around – the movement of the wind, the behavior of animals, the design of the clouds – can offer signs. Dragons often manifest themselves in a veiled way: perhaps in the unexpected flight of a bird, in a ray of sun piercing the trees at the opportune moment, or even in a whisper of the wind among the leaves. Their language is synchronicity, captured by intuition.

The role of dragons in these portals goes beyond simply inhabiting or watching over. They are protectors, activators, and maintainers of the vortexes of force. As protectors, they ensure that the energies remain balanced and that negative or destructive influences do not disturb the sacred place. There are stories of power sites that "repelled" ill-intentioned visitors – from the mystical perspective, it would be the action of the draconic guardian blocking those who could desecrate the place. On the other hand, for those of pure heart or sincere seekers, it is said that the dragon of the place can reveal itself in subtle ways, offering protection and even guidance. As activators, dragons act at key moments, awakening the potential of a portal when the time is right. Ancestral peoples performed ceremonies to "awaken" the spirit of the place: they invoked serpents of light emerging from the earth (that is, the dragon's own energy) to renew fertility and harmony. These rituals suggest that dragons, as expressions of telluric energy, awakened along with the collective consciousness in sacred cycles. Finally, as maintainers, these beings would help regulate the flow of energies over the centuries. Even when a vortex is not evident or is forgotten by people, the guardian dragon remains vigilant, ensuring that the vital pulse continues to flow.

We can imagine them as invisible gardeners of the planetary energy field – trimming excesses, strengthening weakened points, and guiding the flow to maintain balance between Earth and Heaven.

There is no shortage of reports of experiences in portals that people interpret as encounters with dragons. It is not always a clear vision of a winged and scaly being – in fact, it rarely is. Draconic manifestations are usually subtle, perceived with the "inner eye" or in dreams inspired by the stay in a certain sacred place. A traveler who spent the night near Stonehenge reported dreaming of a huge white dragon winding between the stones under a starry sky – upon waking, he felt that he had received a message about the union between heaven and earth. On Mount Shasta, in California, a group of meditators claimed to have seen the outline of a golden dragon forming in the clouds over the snowy peak, followed by a wave of bliss that enveloped them, as if that celestial apparition were blessing them.

There are also experiences of healing and personal transformation attributed to the draconic presence in these places. An Andean healer narrated feeling a strong current running through her spine when meditating on the shores of Lake Titicaca; she visualized a luminous serpent spiraling up her body and, after that, gained deep insights and a sense of spiritual purification, attributing the phenomenon to the blessing of the guardian spirit of the lake. Similarly, pilgrims on Mount Kailash, in Tibet – considered by some traditions as the abode of draconic beings – describe altered states of consciousness during the circumambulation of the mountain. Some report a sudden ecstasy, as if a loving and ancient presence were flooding them. These personal experiences reinforce in those who have them the conviction that dragons are not just metaphors, but subtle realities that inhabit places of power.

As we explore energy portals and the manifestation of dragons, a coherent picture emerges: the Earth, with its network of subtle energies, seems to be permeated by an intelligent consciousness that many cultures have portrayed in the form of the dragon. These beings, at once mythical and real on the spiritual plane, would be expressions of the very soul of the world, connecting sacred places like threads of a great luminous tapestry. Each energy portal would be a knot where the dragon – the conscious energy of the Earth – surfaces to interact with those who are receptive there. Thus, visiting one of these places is not just tourism or curiosity; it can become a transformative encounter with primordial forces. When we walk on ground consecrated by time and the veneration of generations, we are also treading in the wake of dragons. To feel their presence is to access a deeper level of reality, where nature and spirit merge.

In short, the energy portals scattered around the world function as points of contact between our physical world and the subtle dimensions. They are living passageways through which flows the energy that nourishes planetary life and consciousness. And dragons, far from being mere creatures of tale, emerge as guardians and manifesters of these forces. Recognizing this connection invites us to a more reverent relationship with the Earth. It means understanding that each sacred mountain, each mysterious lake, each ancient stone circle is not empty – there may dwell the draconic wisdom, silent, waiting for those who arrive with an open heart and awakened spirit. By respecting and seeking to understand these vortexes and their guardians, we honor the ancient alliance between humanity and dragons, renewing it for the times to come.

Chapter 13
Connecting with Dragons

The connection with dragons happens on a subtle level, accessible only to those who have developed the sensitivity necessary to perceive their presence. These beings do not manifest tangibly in the physical world, but their energy can be felt as a vibrant flow that crosses dimensions and resonates deeply within the soul. This interaction is neither random nor can it be forced; it establishes itself gradually, as the individual expands their perception and attunes to the frequencies that sustain this form of consciousness. Dragons, in their spiritual aspect, are guardians of ancestral knowledge and bearers of a primordial wisdom that transcends time and space. For those seeking this connection, it is essential to cultivate a state of receptivity and respect, understanding that these beings interact only with those who demonstrate sincerity and spiritual maturity.

The draconic presence can be perceived in different ways, depending on the sensitivity of each individual. For some, it manifests as a sensation of intense heat coursing through the body, similar to a subtle electric current that awakens dormant energy centers. For others, it is a state of profound serenity, an inner silence that asserts itself and opens the way for clear intuitions and transformative insights. There are also those who experience this connection through vivid dreams, where dragons appear as guides or protectors, conveying enigmatic messages that become understandable over time. In moments of meditation or introspection, their presence can be felt as an energy field all around, a pulsation that alters the perception of reality and expands consciousness. These manifestations do not follow a fixed pattern, as the way each person interacts with this energy depends on their individual journey and the level of attunement they have achieved.

To establish and strengthen this connection, it is necessary to develop practices that increase energetic perception and affinity with the elements that symbolize the draconic essence. Meditation is one of the most effective paths, allowing the mind to calm down and become receptive to subtle impressions. Visualizing a sacred space – such as a towering mountain, an ancient cave, or an infinite sky – and imagining the presence of a dragon can help create a gradual bond with this energy. In addition, paying attention to signs and synchronicities in daily life can reveal the approach of this force: recurring images of dragons, unexpected encounters with references to these beings, or even changes in the surrounding energy are indications that the connection is forming. Working with the four elements – fire, earth, water, and air – can also facilitate this alignment, as dragons are often associated with the primordial forces of nature. Lighting a flame with intention, feeling the breeze in a moment of contemplation, immersing oneself in natural waters, or walking barefoot on the earth are subtle, yet powerful, ways to create harmony with this ancestral presence. Thus, the connection with dragons is not just an isolated mystical event, but a continuous process of awakening and transformation, which requires dedication, respect, and a sincere search for self-knowledge.

The draconic energy manifests itself in various forms. Some people describe its presence as an intense force, a kind of heat or electricity running through the body, while others perceive it as a wave of serenity and deep wisdom. At certain times, it can be felt as a whisper in the mind, a voice that is neither exactly external nor internal, but which conveys messages with absolute clarity. In other cases, it manifests through vivid dreams, where dragons appear as guides or protectors, transmitting teachings that become more understandable over time.

Many of those who sense the energy of dragons report a subtle change in the environment around them. The air may feel charged, as if it were pulsating, and a sensation of strong, yet not oppressive, presence may arise suddenly. This perception usually happens in moments of introspection or meditation, when the mind is calm and open to receiving these impressions. There are also those who notice the draconic presence in times of great need, when they face internal or external challenges and feel an inexplicable surge of strength and courage, as if something greater were supporting them.

To develop sensitivity to the energy of dragons, it is necessary to cultivate subtle perception and connection with the energetic world. Practices such as meditation and visualization are fundamental to creating a receptive channel for this frequency. During meditation, one can imagine a vast open space, such as an ancient mountain or an untouched valley, and visualize a dragon emerging from this scenery. This image need not be detailed or fixed, as the intuitive mind will fill in the details as the connection strengthens. The more the practice is repeated, the clearer the sensation of presence and interaction will become.

Another way to tune into this energy is to pay attention to the signs that arise in everyday life. Dragons often communicate through synchronicities and symbols that appear repeatedly. Unexpectedly finding images of dragons, hearing stories about them at significant moments, or even feeling inexplicable urges to learn more about their nature can be an indication that this energy is approaching. The more one observes and recognizes these signs, the stronger the bond created will be.

The use of natural elements can also facilitate this connection. Dragons are associated with the four elements – fire, water, earth, and air – and working with these elements in spiritual practices can help anchor their energy. Lighting a candle, immersing oneself in a river or sea, walking barefoot on the earth, or feeling the wind on one's face are simple, yet powerful, ways to align with their forces. Certain stones and crystals, such as obsidian, amethyst, and quartz, are also known to aid in attunement with draconic energies, as they amplify spiritual perception and connection to subtle planes.

Sacred symbols linked to dragons can also serve as anchors for this energy. Many reports indicate that certain symbols, when used in meditations or visualizations, facilitate contact and activation of draconic consciousness. Some of these symbols appear in ancient cultures, such as Chinese glyphs representing celestial dragons or Celtic spirals, which evoke the serpentine movement of primordial energy. Creating or carrying a personal symbol that represents this connection can act as a channeler of its presence in daily life.

There are many documented experiences of people who have felt or interacted with the presence of dragons. Some report unexpected encounters during astral projections, where they felt the imposing presence of a dragon observing them, without words, but transmitting a silent wisdom. Others mention that, in moments of great tension or danger, a sharpened instinct and an inner strength arose as if they came from something beyond themselves, giving them the courage to act. Many spiritualists believe that these experiences are manifestations of draconic energy, which makes itself present to guide, protect, and teach.

The connection with dragons is not something that can be rushed or demanded. It happens organically, as the person becomes more receptive and prepared to deal with this ancestral force. Those who try to invoke dragons with selfish intentions or without due respect rarely manage to establish a real bond. These beings do not respond to superficial desires or mere human whims;

they interact with those who demonstrate a true commitment to their own growth and evolution.

Dragons are guardians of hidden knowledge, and their energy cannot be manipulated without consequences. Therefore, it is essential that any attempt to connect with them be made with sincerity, humility, and a genuine willingness to learn. For those who truly wish to feel their presence, the key is not in the unbridled search, but in the internal preparation. Being aligned with oneself, seeking truth without illusions, and developing intuition are fundamental steps to create this bond.

Feeling the energy of dragons is more than a simple spiritual phenomenon; it is an invitation to transcend the limits of the ordinary mind and access a broader consciousness. It is a call to integrate strength, wisdom, and balance, allowing their presence to guide one's personal journey. Those who open themselves to this experience find not only a deep spiritual contact, but also an inner transformation that resonates in all areas of life.

The connection with dragons is a path of self-knowledge and awakening, where draconic energy becomes part of the individual's very essence. As this connection strengthens, the perception of reality expands, and the world begins to be seen from a new perspective, where everything is interconnected and charged with meaning. Dragons are silent masters who await those who are ready to listen. For those who feel the call, the first step is to open oneself to their presence and allow their energy to flow, guiding them beyond what is visible and awakening truths that have always been hidden, waiting to be rediscovered.

Chapter 14
Dragons as Spiritual Guardians

The presence of dragons as spiritual guardians transcends the boundaries of mythology and enters the very heart of humanity's most ancient esoteric traditions. These entities are not merely symbols of strength and power, but also representations of a higher consciousness that protects, guides, and challenges those on the path of spiritual evolution. Their energy is perceived by those who are ready to access hidden knowledge and face the trials necessary for the expansion of consciousness. Unlike the fierce and destructive image associated with many Western legends, dragons are, in truth, guardians of primordial wisdom, acting as bridges between the material world and higher dimensions. They do not grant their protection indiscriminately; their presence manifests only when there is a true spiritual purpose and a sincere search for understanding the mysteries of existence.

The role of dragons as guardians can manifest in various ways. In some cases, they protect places of intense energetic power, ensuring that only those with spiritual maturity can access these regions. Many cultures around the world report the presence of dragons guarding sacred temples, ancestral mountains, deep caves, and interdimensional portals. These locations are not just physical spaces, but also points of convergence between different layers of reality, where energy is intense and transformative. On an individual level, dragons also act as spiritual guides, assisting those who are undergoing profound internal processes of transformation. Many people who connect with their energy report feeling their presence in crucial moments of life, when great challenges arise or when an important decision needs to be made. In these situations, dragons do not offer ready-made answers, but lead the seeker to find within themselves the courage and wisdom to move forward.

The relationship between dragons and their proteges is not based on submission or dependence, but on mutual growth. They teach that true protection does not come from external barriers, but from inner strengthening. Those who seek this connection must be willing to develop self-confidence, resilience, and discipline. The dragon energy does not protect those who flee from their challenges, but rather those who face their fears with determination and seek balance between power and responsibility. Dragons do not impose their presence on those who are not ready; they wait patiently until the call is made with respect and genuine intention. Those who manage to establish this connection find an invisible force at their side, not to eliminate difficulties, but to provide the necessary support so that they can overcome them on their own. Thus, dragons do not just protect – they shape, transform, and elevate those who prove worthy of their presence, leading them on a path of profound self-knowledge and spiritual awakening.

The role of dragons as guardians can be understood from different perspectives. In some traditions, they protect sacred sites and energy portals, ensuring that only those with spiritual maturity can access these spaces. In others, their function is more individual, serving as guides for those who tread paths of expanding consciousness and face deep internal challenges. In both situations, their presence is perceived not as something that imposes arbitrary barriers, but as a force that demands respect, commitment, and a pure heart to be accessed.

Reports of dragons as protectors appear in various cultures around the world. In the East, celestial dragons are seen as guardians of universal harmony, balancing cosmic forces to ensure the stability of the world. In Japan and China, temples and sacred mountains are often associated with these beings, being considered places where their presence can be felt more intensely. In Tibetan tradition, it is believed that dragons guard sacred texts and hidden teachings, revealing them only to those who are prepared to understand them.

In medieval Europe, dragons were often portrayed as beings that protected treasures hidden in caves or ancient castles. Although many of these stories depict them as hostile creatures, a deeper look reveals that these "treasures" were not just gold and jewels, but rather symbols of forbidden knowledge or spiritual enlightenment. The dragon was not just a monster to be defeated, but rather a challenge that tested the courage and wisdom of those who sought to access such riches. In some versions of these legends, the heroes who faced the dragons did not destroy them, but learned from them, receiving teachings and blessings before continuing their journey.

In shamanism and indigenous traditions, dragons or large winged serpents are considered ancestral spirits that protect tribes and sacred regions. In some South American cultures, it is believed that these beings live in the depths of the forest or in the mountains, watching over those who enter their domains. Shamans and healers report experiences of contact with these entities during altered states of consciousness, where they receive guidance on how to balance energies and heal spiritual imbalances.

The concept of dragons as guardians is also present in contemporary accounts of spiritual experiences. Many people who connect with dragon energy describe a feeling of intense protection, as if an invisible force were accompanying their journeys. Some report vivid dreams where dragons appear as guides, offering advice and warnings about important decisions. Others perceive their presence during moments of great personal transformation, when life seems to be changing drastically and a new path begins to form.

The relationship between dragons and spiritual protection also manifests in the energy field. Some practitioners of magic and spirituality work with dragon energy to create circles of protection, strengthen their auric field, and ward off negative influences. It is believed that dragons possess an extremely high vibration, making it difficult for disharmonious forces to approach when their presence is evoked. In some traditions, specific rituals are performed to ask for their protection, involving the use of symbols, mantras, and symbolic offerings that demonstrate respect and reverence for their presence.

Connecting with dragons as spiritual guardians is not something that can be forced or manipulated. These beings do not respond to invocations made without purpose or to requests driven by ego. Their protection is granted to those who demonstrate sincerity, integrity, and a genuine desire for evolution. Those who try to invoke them for selfish purposes or to obtain power without responsibility usually find silence or, in some cases, experiences that force them to confront their own shadows before proceeding.

Dragons teach that true protection does not come from external barriers, but from inner strengthening. Working with their energy does not only mean seeking security, but learning to develop self-confidence and resilience in the face of life's challenges. They guide those who are ready to face their fears, overcome limitations, and take full responsibility for their spiritual journey. This protection does not manifest as direct intervention, but as a presence that inspires strength and wisdom, helping to find the right path even in the most difficult situations.

Many of those who establish a deep connection with dragons perceive significant changes in their lives. The presence of these guardians can lead to greater mental clarity, the overcoming of destructive patterns, and the awakening of intuitive abilities that were previously dormant. There are reports of people who, after connecting with this energy, began to have more vivid dreams, felt an increased sensitivity to the energies around them, and developed a sharper perception of the intentions of people and the events around them.

The way dragons choose to protect each person varies according to their needs and level of consciousness. For some, their presence may be perceived as a subtle force that wards off negative influences even before they approach. For others, it may manifest as a test, placing challenges in their path so that they strengthen their resilience and ability to make wise decisions. Dragons do not grant protection passively, but teach those who follow them to become their own guardians, taking control of their own energy and destiny.

The spiritual journey under the guidance of dragons is a path of growth and responsibility. For those who feel called to this connection, the first step is to develop a relationship of respect and openness, allowing their presence to reveal itself naturally. This can be done through meditation, observation of signs in daily life, and the practice of introspection. As this relationship deepens, the feeling of protection and guidance becomes clearer, and the teachings of dragons begin to manifest in a more intense and transformative way.

Dragons are guardians of ancient and timeless forces, and their presence in a person's life is a sign that they are ready to tread a path of self-discovery and inner power. They do not impose protection in a paternalistic way, but teach that true security comes from knowledge, courage, and balance. Those who recognize them as guides and learn from their teachings discover a new world, where spiritual strength manifests consciously and responsibly. Dragons do not only guard secrets and ancestral knowledge; they guard those who are ready to awaken to their true essence.

Chapter 15
Evolution of Consciousness

The evolution of human consciousness is a continuous process of expansion and transformation, driven by challenges that demand courage, discernment, and a deep commitment to self-knowledge. In various spiritual traditions, dragons represent this journey, symbolizing both the forces that test the individual and those that guide them toward higher states of perception. These beings, often described as guardians of ancestral wisdom, not only protect hidden knowledge but also act as catalysts for inner change, leading those who are ready to cross the portals of expanded understanding. Their energy manifests as a call to overcome limitations, challenging the mind to break free from old structures and access deeper truths about the nature of reality and the self.

The connection with dragons in the process of conscious evolution doesn't occur in a linear or predictable way. It happens when an individual reaches a point in their journey where their old worldview no longer serves them, and the need for expansion becomes inevitable. This awakening often occurs through intense experiences, whether internal or external, that require the deconstruction of limiting beliefs and the abandonment of obsolete patterns. Dragons, in this context, symbolize the transformative force that drives this change, representing both the challenge and the solution. Their energy acts as an alchemical fire that purifies and strengthens, leading consciousness to higher states of perception. Those who come into contact with this force frequently report increased intuition, enhanced mental clarity, and a deeper connection with the subtle aspects of existence.

More than mere archetypes of power and mystery, dragons reflect a cosmic intelligence that interacts with humanity during moments of great individual and collective transitions. Throughout history, their presence has been associated with periods of disruption and renewal, moments when the collective consciousness is propelled to evolve to new levels. They represent the need for adaptation and growth, teaching that true evolution comes not from resisting change, but from consciously accepting the transformative flow of life. For those who feel the call of this energy, the path opens to a journey of profound self-mastery, where challenges are not obstacles, but opportunities to awaken to a broader and more meaningful reality. Thus, the evolution of consciousness under the influence of dragons is not just a learning process, but an experience of rebirth, where the old dissolves to make way for the new, in an infinite cycle of spiritual expansion and ascension.

The evolution of human consciousness occurs in cycles, driven by experiences that challenge the perception of reality and encourage the individual to question their beliefs and expand their worldview. Dragons play an essential role in this process, as they represent the bridge between hidden knowledge and enlightenment. In some esoteric traditions, they are seen as guardians of cosmic mysteries, beings who test those who wish to access higher levels of understanding. This test, however, does not occur through physical confrontations, as in medieval legends, but through the inner journey that requires courage, detachment, and the willingness to abandon old illusions.

Connecting with draconic energy can accelerate the activation of latent human potential. Like the serpent that symbolizes the awakening of kundalini, dragons are energies that propel the human being to transcend their own limitations. Their presence can be felt by those who are in moments of profound transformation, when old patterns are being destroyed to make way for a new consciousness. Many people report that, upon contacting the energy of dragons, they experience an increase in intuition, an expansion of perception, and an intense sense of purpose. This occurs because these beings act as catalysts for change, helping to dissolve internal blockages and expand spiritual vision.

The influence of dragons on the evolution of consciousness is not restricted to the individual. On a collective level, their energy manifests whenever humanity goes through periods of great transitions. Throughout history, there have been moments when new ideas emerged, challenging established structures and leading to leaps in the understanding of existence. Many spiritualists believe that dragons are present at these moments, influencing the collective consciousness so that the transformation occurs in a more harmonious and accelerated way. Their role, in these cases, is to stimulate the breaking of paradigms, allowing humanity to open up to realities previously considered unattainable.

The symbolism of dragons as agents of change and awakening can be found in various spiritual traditions. In Alchemy, for example, the dragon represents the principle of raw material that needs to be refined and transformed to reach its state of perfection. It is both the destructive force that dissolves impurities and the sacred fire that purifies and elevates. This symbolism reflects the very process of spiritual evolution, in which the human being needs to face their shadows and overcome internal challenges before reaching a higher state of consciousness.

The presence of dragons is also associated with the strengthening of intuition and the opening of new levels of perception. Those who establish a connection with this energy often report an increase in mental clarity and the ability to interpret the subtle signs of the universe. Intuition becomes sharper, allowing decisions to be made with greater confidence and alignment with one's life purpose. In addition, many describe experiences of contact with dragons through dreams, meditations, or moments of spontaneous insight, in which they feel their guidance unmistakably.

Reports of individuals who have had profound experiences with draconic energy are numerous and diverse. Some people describe encounters in meditative states, in which a dragon appears as a guide, conveying messages that resonate on a deep level. Others claim that their connection with dragons has helped them overcome fears, face seemingly insurmountable challenges, and rediscover their own inner strength. There are also those who report feeling an invisible protection in moments of danger or transition, as if an ancestral presence were watching over them.

Those who actively seek connection with dragons to aid in their evolutionary process must be prepared for significant changes. Draconic energy is not subtle or complacent; it demands commitment and a willingness to grow. Unlike other forms of spiritual guidance, dragons do not lead the way with gentleness, but with the force necessary for transformation to occur in a profound and true way. Their main teaching is that of self-reliance, courage, and the tireless pursuit of truth.

The role of dragons in the evolution of consciousness is not limited to an abstract or symbolic concept. Those who feel their presence know that their energy is real and can be worked with in a practical way in everyday life. Integrating the wisdom of dragons means learning to face challenges without fear, developing discernment to perceive what is essential, and acting with determination to manifest positive changes. They teach that spiritual evolution is not a path of escape, but a journey of self-mastery and inner strengthening.

As more people awaken to the reality beyond the visible, the influence of dragons on human consciousness is likely to become more evident. Their return to collective memory is not a coincidence, but a sign that humanity is ready to access deeper levels of wisdom. More and more individuals report feeling their presence and learning from their energy, indicating that these beings are once again becoming active allies in the process of planetary ascension.

Dragons are not just figures of ancient legends, but living forces that continue to influence those who are ready to receive them. Their role in the evolution of consciousness is to challenge, awaken, and strengthen. They are present whenever a soul is ready to transcend its limitations and embrace its true nature. Working with their energy is not a path for the faint of heart, but for those who have the courage to look within themselves and accept the transformation necessary to evolve.

The call of the dragons resonates with those who possess an indomitable spirit and a genuine search for truth. They do not appear to those who seek shortcuts or easy rewards, but to those who are willing to walk the path of enlightenment with integrity and determination. For those who feel this connection, the journey is just the beginning. The presence of the dragons indicates that the soul is ready to awaken to its true essence and tread a path of power, wisdom, and profound transformation.

Chapter 16
Dragons and Kundalini Energy

The connection between dragons and Kundalini energy manifests as a profound link between mythical symbolism and the energetic reality present within human beings. Dragons are universal archetypes of power, transformation, and hidden knowledge, representing primordial forces that can both protect and challenge those who dare to awaken their true essence. Kundalini energy, often described as a serpent coiled at the base of the spine, is a latent force that, when activated, travels through the body's energy centers, promoting expanded consciousness and inner transmutation. The relationship between the two is not merely metaphorical; it reflects a reality experienced by those undergoing spiritual awakening, where powerful forces are unleashed, requiring balance, discipline, and understanding to be properly integrated. Just as the dragons of legend guard hidden treasures in deep caverns, Kundalini safeguards within the human being a potential for enlightenment that awaits the right moment to emerge, leading to a journey of self-discovery and elevation.

The ascent of Kundalini is comparable to the hero's journey, who confronts and eventually tames the dragon. In myths, the confrontation with the dragon symbolizes not just an external battle, but an internal process of overcoming fears, emotional purification, and integration of one's own shadow. Similarly, the awakening of Kundalini requires the individual to face unresolved aspects of their psyche, allowing this force to ascend in a balanced way, without generating physical, emotional, or spiritual imbalances. If awakened abruptly or without adequate preparation, this energy can trigger turbulence, manifesting as existential crises, intensification of traumas, or even overwhelming physical sensations. However, when activated consciously and progressively, Kundalini provides mental clarity, expanded perception, and alignment with higher dimensions of existence. In this context, the dragon is not an enemy to be defeated, but a manifestation of one's own inner power that needs to be understood and directed toward a higher purpose.

The presence of dragons in mythologies and esoteric traditions around the world reinforces their connection with Kundalini as a cosmic force regulating life. In the East, dragons are often associated with vital energy, called Qi, which circulates through the body and the universe, sustaining the harmony of natural cycles. In Hinduism, the cosmic serpent Shesha represents the primordial energy that supports existence, reflecting the hidden nature of Kundalini. In the West, the image of the dragon guarding hidden treasures refers to the latent spiritual potential within each individual, a power that needs to be awakened with wisdom to reveal its true grandeur. Thus, the relationship between dragons and

Kundalini transcends allegories and manifests as a universal principle, where the awakening of vital energy is a call to transformation, requiring courage, balance, and preparation so that its force is used in a constructive and enlightening way.

In many cultures, the dragon symbolizes the primordial force, the raw energy of the universe that needs to be refined and directed towards a higher purpose. The parallel between the dragon and Kundalini is not just metaphorical, but a real energetic correspondence perceived by those who have gone through processes of spiritual awakening. Like the dragon, Kundalini can be an agent of destruction or enlightenment, depending on how it is awakened and guided. When activated in a balanced way, this energy brings clarity, expanded perception, and spiritual alignment. However, if awakened without proper preparation, it can generate emotional turbulence, disorientation, and even existential crises.

Dragons represent the upward movement of Kundalini and its transformation along the chakras. In the initial stage, the energy is dormant, symbolized by the dragon asleep in caves or hidden places, waiting for the right moment to awaken. When activated, the energy rises through the spine, awakening each energy center and bringing changes in various aspects of life. This process is similar to the hero's journey of facing a dragon: it is not about destroying it, but about learning to master and integrate it.

The activation of Kundalini is often described as a sensation of intense heat rising through the spine, accompanied by profound insights, greater energetic sensitivity, and changes in the perception of reality. Some people report that, during this process, they had visions of dragons, either in dreams, meditative states, or even as fleeting visual impressions in the waking world. These accounts suggest that dragons may act as guides or symbolic manifestations of this ascending life force.

The connection between dragons and Kundalini can also be observed in mythology and esoteric traditions. In the East, dragons are often portrayed as celestial forces associated with enlightenment and wisdom. In Taoism, the dragon is a symbol of the vital energy called Qi, which circulates through the body and the universe, regulating the cycles of life. In Hinduism, the cosmic serpent Shesha, upon whom Vishnu rests, is a clear representation of this latent energy that sustains existence. In the Western tradition, the figure of the dragon guarding treasures and caves can be seen as a metaphor for the hidden spiritual energy within the human being, which needs to be awakened and consciously integrated.

Many people who have experienced the awakening of Kundalini report feeling an intense presence, something that cannot be described as just impersonal energy, but as a conscious force, almost like an observing being. There are those who describe the sensation of an invisible gaze, as if an entity were accompanying the process. In some cases, dreams with dragons appear precisely at these moments of transition, as if the Kundalini energy assumed this symbolic form to communicate with the individual's psyche.

Working with Kundalini requires balance, as its activation awakens both luminous aspects and internal shadows that need to be faced. The dragon is a symbol of this duality: it can be destructive when its force is ignored or used recklessly, but it is also a master for those who understand its true nature. Like a winged dragon that rises to the heavens, Kundalini, when guided correctly, elevates consciousness to higher levels, allowing the individual to have deeper spiritual experiences and an expanded understanding of reality.

To awaken and work with this energy safely, it is essential to adopt practices that promote balance and gradual preparation. Meditations focused on conscious breathing and chakra alignment help to stabilize the energy before it begins to ascend. Visualization techniques, where one imagines a serpent or a dragon rising up the spine, can assist in directing this force consciously. The use of specific yoga postures, such as asanas that activate the root chakra and the crown chakra, is also recommended to harmonize this energy and avoid imbalances.

Another fundamental aspect is emotional and mental purification. Kundalini energy amplifies everything that already exists within the individual, both positive aspects and unresolved blocks. Therefore, those who wish to awaken this force must first work on clearing traumas, limiting beliefs, and repressed emotions. Many reports of difficult experiences with Kundalini occur because the energy encounters internal obstacles and needs to break them abruptly, which can generate emotional or physical crises.

In addition to individual practices, connecting with dragons as archetypes can be a powerful tool in this process. Some traditions teach that invoking the draconic energy before meditation or consciousness expansion practices can bring protection and guidance. This can be done through simple rituals, such as lighting candles or incense while visualizing the presence of a guardian dragon, asking that this force assist in harmonizing the Kundalini energy.

There are also those who perceive dragons as manifestations of Kundalini itself at different stages of development. In the beginning, the image of a terrestrial dragon may appear, robust and still connected to the material plane, representing the initial awakening of the energy. As the process progresses, the dragon may appear winged, symbolizing the ascent through the higher centers of consciousness. In the final stage, it may appear as an entity of pure light, representing the complete fusion between matter and spirit.

The relationship between dragons and Kundalini is not just an esoteric concept, but an experience lived by many who tread paths of spiritual awakening. The presence of dragons in this process reinforces the idea that the awakening of consciousness is not just an energetic phenomenon, but an event that involves deep archetypes of the collective unconscious. The dragon is not only a symbol of strength and power, but also a guide for those who are ready to cross the portals of transformation.

Kundalini energy is the key to accessing higher dimensions of existence, but its awakening requires responsibility and preparation. Dragons, as guardians of this force, teach that true power lies not in forcing evolution, but in allowing it to occur naturally and balanced. Working with this energy is making a commitment to one's own expansion of consciousness and being willing to face everything that needs to be transmuted.

The path of Kundalini is the journey of the dragon: a crossing of challenges and discoveries that leads to the awakening of the true essence. Those who hear the call of this ancestral power and honor it with respect find not only transformation, but a new meaning for their existence. The dragon of Kundalini does not destroy to punish, but to reveal what has always been hidden, waiting to be understood and integrated into the light of awakened consciousness.

Chapter 17
Dragons and the Protection of the Planet

The presence of dragons in the balance of the planet is not limited to the realm of mythology, but manifests as an energetic principle that transcends cultures and eras. These beings, often associated with the primordial elements of nature, play an essential role in maintaining the harmony of the environment and the Earth's energy flows. Since the earliest civilizations, there have been accounts of dragons as guardians of rivers, mountains, and forests, representing forces that regulate life and ensure the continuity of natural cycles. Their connection to ecosystems is not merely symbolic; many spiritual traditions believe that these beings act on subtle planes, sustaining the vitality of sacred places and protecting the purity of natural resources. They are seen as entities of great wisdom, whose mission is directly connected to preserving planetary balance, ensuring that natural forces flow harmoniously, and that humanity understands its responsibility in protecting the Earth.

The connection between dragons and the elements of nature reinforces the idea that their presence is intrinsically linked to the functioning of environmental systems. Earth dragons, for example, are described as guardians of telluric forces, those who maintain the planet's geological stability and oversee the flows of underground energy. In various cultures, mountains and caves are considered the dwellings of these beings, places where the Earth's energy is most intense and requires special protection. Water dragons, on the other hand, are associated with the planet's life sources, ensuring the purity of rivers, lakes, and oceans. In several traditions, pollution and the destruction of aquatic ecosystems are interpreted as signs of the withdrawal of dragonic energy, leaving these places vulnerable to imbalance and degradation. Fire dragons, in turn, represent the principle of transmutation and renewal. Although often associated with destruction, they fulfill an essential function in the regeneration of ecosystems, as occurs in natural fires which, despite being devastating, contribute to soil fertilization and the renewal of life. Finally, air dragons symbolize the movement and circulation of vital energies, regulating climate patterns and promoting harmony between the elements. Their influence is present in winds, storms, and the subtlety of seasonal changes, reflecting the balance necessary for the continuation of existence on Earth.

The role of dragons in protecting the planet is not limited to natural forces, but also involves interaction with those who seek to reconnect with the Earth's consciousness. Many people report spiritual experiences in which they feel the presence of these beings while meditating in places of high energetic vibration, such as untouched forests, isolated mountains, or near large bodies of water. These experiences suggest that dragons are not just mythological figures, but intelligences that remain active in subtle dimensions, assisting those who are committed to preserving life and the planet's balance. To establish a deeper connection with these forces, practices such as meditation in natural environments, rituals of gratitude to the elements, and the cultivation of an ecological consciousness are essential. The mission of dragons is not only to protect the Earth, but also to awaken in humanity the understanding that everyone is part of this same living system. Honoring the presence of these forces means recognizing the sacredness of nature and acting responsibly, adopting sustainable practices and respecting natural cycles. When humanity finally understands this interdependence, it can act in partnership with these ancestral forces, becoming, like the dragons, a guardian of life and planetary balance.

The relationship between dragons and the Earth is as old as the planet itself. Different spiritual traditions report that these beings have an active role in maintaining the energetic balance of nature. In the East, dragons are considered spirits of nature, linked to rivers, mountains, and forests. In China, the celestial dragon symbolizes the flow of vital energy that runs through the Earth, responsible for regulating the cycle of the seasons and the fertility of the soil. This same vision can be found in shamanic mythologies, where large winged serpents are seen as protectors of the secrets of the forest and natural cycles.

The idea that dragons act as guardians of the planet is also reflected in the legends that speak of their relationship with sacred energy points. Many places of power around the world, such as towering mountains, deep caves, and isolated islands, are traditionally associated with a draconic presence. It is said that these places hold a special energy, as if they were vortexes of force that sustain the planet's balance. Some mystics claim that these energy points are maintained by dragons, who protect their vibration and prevent disharmonious forces from interfering in these subtle fields.

Earth dragons, in particular, are considered primarily responsible for protecting the planetary ecosystem. Their presence is associated with geological stability and the maintenance of the telluric forces that run through the planet. There are records of ancient cultures that believed that great dragons rested beneath the mountains and that their movements could influence seismic activity. Although this view has been interpreted symbolically by modern science, in esotericism this idea represents the flow of underground energies that feed life on the surface.

In the case of water dragons, their influence is linked to the purification and preservation of natural sources. In various mythologies, they appear as beings that inhabit lakes, rivers, and oceans, protecting the purity of these waters and ensuring that their cycles remain harmonious. Some traditions suggest that when a body of water is polluted or destroyed, the draconic energy withdraws from that place, leaving it vulnerable to even greater degradation. This belief reinforces the idea that environmental preservation is not just a physical issue, but also an energetic one.

Fire dragons, in turn, symbolize transformation and regeneration. In many traditions, they are seen as forces that renew life, destroying what is no longer needed to make way for the new. Their role in protecting the planet is related to the purification of energies and the transmutation of negative influences. Some cultures interpret natural fires that occur in forests as manifestations of this energy, because, despite the initial destruction, these events often result in the rebirth of vegetation and the strengthening of the soil.

Air dragons are the messengers of planetary balance, acting in the circulation of energy currents and in maintaining harmony between the different elements. They are often associated with wind and climate change, being considered regulators of the invisible forces that keep the Earth alive. In some traditions, it is believed that these dragons communicate with those who are attuned to nature, transmitting messages about planetary cycles and the adjustments needed to maintain balance.

The connection between dragons and the protection of the planet is not just a mythological issue, but also a call for humanity to assume its role as guardian of the Earth. Many of the legends that speak of dragons protecting nature contain a profound teaching about the need to respect and preserve the environment. In various traditions, there are stories of dragons that withdrew from certain places due to the destruction caused by human beings, indicating that their presence is directly linked to the harmony between humanity and nature.

Currently, there are many people who feel the presence of these beings in moments of deep connection with nature. Meditators and spiritual practitioners report experiences where they perceive the draconic energy in untouched forests, isolated mountains, or beside large bodies of water. Some describe feelings of protection and strength, as if they were being watched by an ancient and wise consciousness. Others claim to receive intuitive messages about the importance of protecting certain places and maintaining a more balanced relationship with the environment.

For those who wish to align themselves with the mission of dragons in protecting the planet, some practices can be adopted. Meditating in natural places and establishing an intention to connect with the Earth's energy can open channels for this interaction. Performing rituals of gratitude to nature, such as symbolic offerings of flowers or crystals, demonstrates respect for these forces and strengthens the bond with the draconic consciousness. Working directly with the elements – lighting a candle to honor fire, purifying oneself in a water source, feeling the energy of the earth under one's feet, and breathing deeply the pure air – are simple, yet powerful, ways to integrate this connection into daily life.

The mission of dragons in protecting the planet is also a reminder that humanity has an active role in this process. Caring for the environment, reducing the degradation of natural resources, and promoting a more sustainable lifestyle are practical ways to collaborate with this mission. Draconic energy manifests not only in spiritual experiences, but also in the conscious action of those who seek to preserve life and the balance of the Earth.

Dragons are living forces that sustain the planet, ensuring that its natural cycle continues to flow. Their presence may be subtle, but it is always active, protecting the places where the Earth's energy pulses with greater intensity. For those who feel their call, the invitation is clear: to integrate into this mission and become, like the dragons, a guardian of planetary harmony. The protection of the Earth is not the exclusive responsibility of these spiritual forces, but a shared task among all beings who are part of it. When humanity recognizes this truth, perhaps the dragons will fully return, revealing themselves not only as myths of the past, but as allies in the future of the Earth.

Chapter 18
Dragons in Magic and Rituals

Dragon magic is a path of profound power and transformation, accessible only to those who possess the respect, dedication, and spiritual preparedness to interact with ancestral forces of great magnitude. Dragons, far from being mere legendary creatures, are considered guardians of hidden knowledge and the primordial energies of the universe. Their role in magic transcends mythology, as they represent mastery over the elements, the transmutation of the spirit, and the pursuit of ancestral wisdom. Working with dragon magic demands commitment, for their energy is neither passive nor indulgent; it challenges, strengthens, and teaches through direct and intense experiences. Those who seek their connection must be willing to confront their own essence, refine their weaknesses, and transform themselves to handle the indomitable force of these entities.

The rituals involving dragons are not simple esoteric formalities, but sacred processes that establish a channel between the practitioner and the draconic forces. Throughout history, various traditions have described specific methods for invoking and interacting with these beings, varying according to culture and the magician's intention. In the East, Taoist priests used symbols and mantras to honor dragons, seeking balance and protection for their communities. In the West, the Hermetic and alchemical traditions saw dragons as symbols of the great mystery of creation, forces that guarded the secrets of spiritual transmutation and mastery of the elements. Each dragon possesses a unique vibration and operates within a specific field: fire dragons promote courage and transformation, water dragons aid in intuition and emotional purification, earth dragons ensure stability and strength, while air dragons stimulate the mind and the expansion of consciousness. The correct invocation of these beings requires vibrational alignment, well-structured rituals, and a clear intention, as their presence can be overwhelming for those who are not prepared for the intensity of their energy.

The relationship between magicians and dragons is not based on submission or selfish requests, but on mutual learning and respect. Dragons do not allow themselves to be manipulated or subjected to trivial human wills. They teach self-sufficiency, discipline, and inner strength, guiding practitioners through challenges that propel their spiritual growth. Reports of contact with these entities often include vivid dreams, visions during meditations, and intense energetic manifestations, such as changes in ambient temperature, a sense of a powerful presence, or profound insights into personal and universal matters. Working with dragon magic means treading a path of continuous transformation, where the practitioner must prove their determination and integrity before receiving any knowledge or assistance from these forces. Those who manage to establish a true connection with dragons discover that they are not only guardians of knowledge, but also faithful allies on the spiritual journey, ready to guide, protect, and reveal deep secrets about the universe and the very essence of being.

In ancient times, many civilizations had cults dedicated to the veneration of draconic beings. In the East, dragons were considered manifestations of the cosmic flow of vital energy and were associated with the harmony of the elements. Taoist priests performed rituals to honor dragons and seek their aid in protecting harvests and balancing natural forces. In the West, alchemists and occultists saw dragons as guardians of hidden knowledge, responsible for testing those who sought the wisdom of the great mysteries. Hermetic texts mention that the essence of the dragon is the very force of creation, a raw energy that needs to be refined and understood to become an ally on the spiritual journey.

Dragons can be invoked and worked with in rituals for different purposes. In protection practices, their energy can be used to create powerful energy barriers, warding off undesirable influences and strengthening the practitioner's auric field. For healing, their presence can be requested to work on unblocking energy centers and restoring vitality. In processes of transformation, dragons help to break old patterns, bringing courage and strength to face profound changes. Their presence is not subtle, and those who work with them frequently report an intense feeling of power and renewal when performing such rituals.

To establish an effective connection with dragons, certain symbols and tools can be employed. The use of colored candles, especially in red, gold, and blue hues, is common in draconic rituals, as these colors represent strength, wisdom, and protection. Crystals such as obsidian, smoky quartz, and amethyst are also used to tune into the energy of dragons, as they possess properties that aid in expanding perception and anchoring spiritual force. Talismans and specific sigils can be drawn on parchments or carved in stones, serving as channels for the manifestation of the draconic presence during magical practices.

Invoking dragons requires preparation and seriousness. These beings do not respond to trivial calls or superficial intentions. Before performing any ritual, it is essential that the practitioner be in a state of concentration and respect, recognizing the magnitude of the energy with which they wish to work. Many reports from magicians who tried to evoke dragons without proper preparation indicate that such experiences can be overwhelming or even uncomfortable, as draconic energy is intense and requires vibrational alignment. Therefore, meditation and strengthening the personal energy field are fundamental steps before any contact.

One of the most traditional methods of invocation involves creating a circle of energy, where the practitioner traces a sacred space and calls the dragons into this vortex. This process may include the intonation of mantras or words of power that resonate with the draconic frequency. Some esoteric schools teach that the names of dragons vary according to their elemental nature and that each type of dragon has a distinct vibrational pattern, and must be called in a specific way for its energy to be accessed correctly.

In addition to invocation, communication with dragons can occur through dreams and visions. Many practitioners report that, after establishing an initial connection, dragons manifest spontaneously during sleep, transmitting symbolic messages or guidance on the spiritual path. In some traditions, it is believed that dragons choose those with whom they wish to work, and not the other way around. This means that, even if a practitioner wishes to connect with these energies, the response will depend on the degree of attunement and commitment demonstrated over time.

Working with dragon magic also involves responsibility. Unlike other forms of magic, which can be more subtle and accessible, the energy of dragons can be transformative and, at times, challenging. Those who seek their guidance must be prepared to deal with profound changes and teachings that can be uncomfortable. Dragons do not grant favors freely; they teach self-sufficiency and inner strength. Their teachings often involve challenges that lead to spiritual growth and personal strengthening.

Ethics when working with dragons is a crucial aspect. Unlike other spiritual entities that may act in a compassionate and patient manner, dragons demand that their laws be respected. Trying to manipulate their energy for selfish purposes or using their power irresponsibly can bring unexpected consequences. Experienced magicians emphasize that dragons do not tolerate disrespect and that their presence must be honored with humility and sincerity. Requests made improperly or with dishonest intentions are generally not answered, and in some cases, the practitioner may feel a kind of "energetic repulsion," preventing the connection from being established.

There are numerous reports of magical experiences involving dragons. Some practitioners describe feeling the presence of a large being observing them during rituals, while others claim to have seen shadows or luminous forms around them. There are also those who report intense physical sensations, such as a sudden increase in body temperature or a feeling of heaviness in the environment, indicating the draconic manifestation. In some more advanced experiences, practitioners claim to have received direct instructions from dragons, teachings about the nature of reality, or even glimpses of past lives connected to these entities.

Dragon magic is a path that requires commitment, respect, and courage. Those who tread this path discover that dragons are not just mythological beings, but living forces that can act as spiritual guides and allies. Their presence brings strength, discernment, and a sense of deep connection with the mysteries of the universe. More than simply invoking them to obtain favors, the true purpose of working with dragons is personal transformation and the integration of their wisdom into the practitioner's evolutionary journey.

The call of dragons in magic and rituals is not for everyone. It resonates only with those who have the willingness to face challenges and learn from an intense and relentless energy. Working with dragons is not a path for the weak or impatient, but for those who seek a deeper understanding of life, power, and the responsibility that comes with true knowledge. For those who accept this call, the journey is one of profound evolution, where dragons become not only guardians, but masters and allies in the great dance of the universe.

Chapter 19
Encounters with Dragons

Encounters with dragons on the spiritual plane transcend the boundaries of myth and imagination, manifesting as profound experiences that significantly impact those who experience them. These encounters occur in expanded states of consciousness, such as lucid dreams, deep meditations, and astral projections, where dragons emerge as guardians of knowledge, messengers of transformation, and spiritual protectors. Their appearances are not mere constructs of the subconscious mind, but rather events that resonate at the soul level, carrying teachings and challenges designed to awaken hidden potentials. For many, the presence of a dragon is not just a symbolic vision, but a real interaction with a primordial force that assists in the journey of self-discovery, demanding courage and a willingness to confront profound truths.

In dreams, dragons often appear in imposing settings, such as sacred mountains, caves illuminated by crystals, or vast ethereal landscapes, suggesting that these experiences transcend the realm of the unconscious and access higher spiritual dimensions. In these encounters, they may act as silent observers, assessing the dreamer's energy before establishing direct communication, or as guides who lead to discoveries about one's own essence. Some people report that dragons speak through telepathy, transmitting messages encoded in symbols and emotions, while others describe clear dialogues, where they receive advice about their spiritual journey. Beyond dreams, meditation is another powerful means of accessing these beings. Many practitioners report that, upon reaching a deep state of relaxation and focus, they begin to perceive the presence of a dragon as a warm and enveloping energy or as a majestic visual form that conveys strength and wisdom.

Those who experience these encounters often notice changes in their perception and energy after the contact. The presence of a dragon can trigger an inner awakening, leading to greater clarity about one's life purpose and strengthening the connection with one's personal power. Subtle signs begin to appear in everyday life, such as recurring images of dragons in books, art, or subsequent dreams, reinforcing the continuity of this bond. Some individuals report intense synchronicities, such as encountering references to dragons at decisive moments or feeling a protective presence in challenging situations. These encounters are not just isolated events, but mark the beginning of a profound transformation, where the dragon becomes a spiritual mentor who guides, challenges, and strengthens those who are ready to tread the path of evolution and awakening.

Dreams are one of the most frequent ways in which dragons manifest. Many people report that, in moments of great personal transformation or when seeking answers to internal dilemmas, dragons appear in their dreams with an imposing presence, communicating through images, symbols, or, in some cases, through telepathic words. These encounters often occur in grandiose landscapes, such as colossal mountains, caves filled with crystals, or floating realms, suggesting that such visions belong to higher dimensions or ancestral records of the soul.

There are those who describe the presence of a dragon observing them from a distance, as if testing their courage and willingness to learn. In other accounts, dragons appear close by, guiding dreamers through unknown paths, showing visions of past lives, or teaching lessons about balance and inner strength. Some experiences report that dragons appear to assist in confronting deep-seated fears, symbolizing the need to face internal challenges before moving forward on the spiritual journey.

Beyond dreams, many people report encounters with dragons during deep meditative states. Through practices of breathing, visualization, and focus, some are able to feel their presence intensely, perceiving vivid images, waves of energy, or a sensation of warmth and protection around them. During these meditations, some describe seeing dragons of vibrant colors that seem to communicate telepathically, conveying messages about their personal journey and offering insights into the present moment. For many, these experiences are transformative, generating a new understanding of themselves and their life purpose.

Another way in which encounters with dragons occur is through astral projection. Experienced astral travelers report being guided by dragons through dimensional portals, accessing unknown realms and absorbing profound teachings. Some claim that dragons act as protectors in these planes, ensuring that the projected soul does not stray into low-vibration zones or become influenced by negative entities. In some cases, dragons seem to act as guardians of hidden knowledge, testing those who wish to access certain records and allowing their entry only when they deem the seeker ready.

The nature of these interactions varies according to the spiritual maturity and level of consciousness of the individual. For some, dragons appear symbolically, representing internal aspects that need to be worked on, such as courage, determination, or the mastery of primitive impulses. For others, the encounters seem to be real experiences in higher spiritual planes, where these beings act as guides and transmitters of cosmic teachings. The line between the symbolic and the real may be thin, but the impact of these experiences on the lives of those who experience them is undeniable.

The signs left by dragons after these encounters can manifest in various forms in the physical world. Some people report unexpectedly finding images of dragons, whether in books, paintings, or sculptures, as if the universe were reinforcing the presence of this archetype in their lives. Others perceive changes in their personal energy, feeling stronger, more protected, or with greater mental clarity after an encounter with a dragon in a dream or meditation. There are also reports of synchronicities, where information about dragons begins to appear repeatedly in daily life, suggesting a call to deepen this connection.

Interpreting these signs requires sensitivity and introspection. Each experience is unique and carries a personal meaning for the one who experiences it. To understand a dragon's message, it is important to reflect on the context of the encounter, the emotions felt, and the teachings transmitted. In some cases, dragons appear to warn about choices or paths to be taken, while in others, they emerge as confirmation that the individual is on the right track. Regardless of how they manifest, these encounters leave a lasting mark and awaken a new level of consciousness in those who experience them.

The impact of these encounters on spiritual awakening is profound. Many who undergo these experiences report an expansion of their perception of reality, feeling more connected to the universe and the subtle energies that permeate it. The presence of a dragon can signify a call for inner transformation, an invitation to overcome fears and expand the understanding of one's own existence. Some individuals begin to develop more acute intuitive abilities after these encounters, feeling a greater ease in capturing subtle messages or perceiving the energy around them with more clarity.

Reports of encounters with dragons suggest that these beings act as catalysts for spiritual evolution. Their energy, powerful and imposing, does not allow for illusions or escapism. When they appear in someone's life, they bring with them a call for that person to face their truth, embrace their strength, and walk with courage towards self-knowledge. Unlike other forms of spiritual guidance, which may be gentler and more compassionate, dragons challenge those they encounter to take full responsibility for their journey.

For those seeking this type of contact, the key lies in openness and sincere intention. Working on the connection with dragons requires patience, respect, and a willingness to learn. The practice of meditation, the study of draconic symbols, and the observation of signs in daily life are ways to strengthen this connection and allow these beings to manifest more clearly. Dragons do not appear by chance; their presence is a reflection of the spiritual readiness of those who encounter them.

Encounters with dragons, whether symbolic or spiritual, are always striking and transformative. They represent an invitation to look beyond the visible, expand the horizons of consciousness, and embrace the journey of awakening with strength and determination. Those who accept this call discover that dragons are not just figures from ancient legends, but living forces that continue to operate on the subtle plane, guiding and challenging those who are ready to tread the path of wisdom and spiritual evolution.

Chapter 20
The Draconic Bloodlines

Draconic bloodlines represent a spiritual inheritance that transcends myths and legends, manifesting as a real and powerful presence in the journey of certain souls. The connection with dragons is not limited to symbolic figures or psychological archetypes; it is a deep energetic resonance, rooted in ancestral memories and vibrational patterns that span incarnations. Since time immemorial, some spiritual lineages have maintained a link with these primordial entities, whose influence shapes both the character and the life mission of those who carry them. This affinity manifests through an unwavering inner strength, an innate sense of leadership, and a relentless pursuit of hidden knowledge and spiritual transcendence. Those who belong to this lineage often feel, from childhood, that they do not entirely fit into the conventional structures of society, as if they carry within them a call to something grand and hidden. It is a sense of belonging to something beyond the visible, a bond with forces that surpass the limits of ordinary human understanding.

The awakening to this connection can occur in various ways. Some people experience recurring dreams in which they interact with dragons, receiving teachings or protection. Others feel an inexplicable attraction to stories, symbols, and representations of these entities, as if a latent memory were triggered upon contact with such references. There are also those who perceive this influence in their own behavior and characteristics, possessing a personality marked by courage, determination, and a strong protective instinct, as if carrying the spirit of an ancestral guardian. Furthermore, the connection with the natural elements – especially fire, earth, water, and air – can indicate the presence of a draconic bond, as dragons are traditionally associated with these primordial forces. This elemental connection can manifest in sensitivity to energy changes in the environment, ease in working with magic or energy healing, and the ability to influence the surrounding vibration. These signs point to a spiritual heritage that transcends individuality, connecting the individual to an ancient and sacred legacy.

Understanding and accepting this lineage is a process of self-discovery and spiritual deepening. Draconic energy is not granted arbitrarily; it demands discipline, honor, and a genuine commitment to inner growth. Meditation and practices of connection with dragons are effective ways to awaken this awareness, allowing the person to receive insights and guidance directly from these entities. Working with symbols and practices associated with dragons can strengthen the attunement, helping to unlock latent memories and abilities. Furthermore, exploring mythology and historical records about dragons can provide valuable clues about how this energy manifests throughout the ages and how it influences those who carry it. The draconic call is not just a distant memory of a lost past, but an invitation to take an active role in spiritual and collective transformation. Those who respond to this call become beacons of wisdom and strength, guided by a lineage that echoes through time, challenging the limits of the ordinary and revealing the grandeur of a legacy that has never been extinguished.

Draconic lineages are often associated with individuals who demonstrate characteristics such as unwavering willpower, sharp intuition, and a very clear sense of mission. People who possess this connection often feel from an early age that they do not entirely belong to the ordinary world, carrying an intense desire to unravel mysteries, explore spiritual dimensions, and understand realities beyond what the physical eyes can see. In some traditions, it is believed that these souls may have incarnated in periods of history where dragons were more present in human consciousness, or even that they possess energetic records that refer to ancient civilizations where interaction with dragons was direct and respected.

The concept of spiritual DNA suggests that certain memories and vibrational patterns can be transmitted from one incarnation to another, preserving the essence and mission of a spirit throughout different lives. For those who possess a draconic heritage, this influence manifests as an inner call, an almost irresistible need to seek hidden knowledge, protect sacred truths, or even act as spiritual guides and leaders.

This energetic DNA is not something physical, but a vibrational pattern that resonates with the energy of dragons, creating a natural attunement between the individual and these ancestral forces.

There are several signs that can indicate a spiritual connection with dragons. One of the most common is the persistent feeling of familiarity when hearing stories about these beings or when coming into contact with draconic symbols. Some people feel an inexplicable attraction to images of dragons, to mythologies that involve them, or to spiritual practices that work with their energy. Others report recurring dreams in which they interact with dragons in different ways, whether as allies, teachers, or protectors.

Another strong indicator of this connection is the presence of natural abilities related to energy and intuition. Individuals of draconic lineage tend to be highly perceptive, able to pick up on subtleties in the environment and in the emotions of people around them. They also tend to have a magnetic presence, conveying authority and strength even without needing to impose their will. Many report an innate connection with the elements, feeling a special affinity with fire, earth, water, or air, which can indicate a connection with different types of dragons.

The influence of this spiritual heritage on one's life mission is significant. Those who possess a draconic lineage generally feel a greater purpose that drives them to seek knowledge, transformation, and leadership. Many end up following spiritual paths, becoming teachers, healers, mages, or guardians of sacred knowledge. Others manifest this energy in more practical areas, acting as protectors of nature, defenders of just causes, or leaders who inspire profound changes in society.

To discover and awaken this connection, a process of self-knowledge and spiritual exploration is necessary. Meditation is a fundamental tool, as it allows access to ancient memories and understanding of one's own spiritual identity. Guided visualizations can help to contact the energy of dragons, allowing their presence to reveal itself in a gradual and respectful way. The study of mythologies and symbolic systems can also offer clues about this connection, helping the individual to identify patterns and references that resonate with their essence.

Furthermore, working with the elements can strengthen this connection. For those who feel an affinity with fire dragons, practices involving candles, rituals of transmutation, and work with the energy of will can be extremely effective. Those who connect more with water dragons can explore intuition through meditation with water sources, ritual baths, and practices of emotional purification. Those who resonate with earth dragons can seek this energy in outdoor rituals, contact with crystals, and work with grounding and stability. And for those who feel the presence of air dragons, practices such as the use of incense, chanting mantras, and meditations for expanding consciousness can be effective means of attuning to this vibration.

Reports from people who have discovered this connection show how this revelation can completely transform someone's life. Many describe that, after understanding their draconic lineage, they began to have greater clarity about their purpose, feeling more aligned with their true essence. Some mention that, upon accepting this connection, they began to receive clearer messages during dreams or intuitions, as if the dragons were guiding them on their journey. Others report that they felt a significant increase in energy and vitality, as if an ancient blockage had been removed and their true strength could finally manifest.

The relationship between draconic lineages and spiritual awakening goes beyond a symbolic identification. For those who truly possess this connection, the energy of dragons becomes a guide, an impulse to evolve, challenge limits, and expand horizons. These individuals often realize that their journey is not just personal, but that they are part of a larger movement, a collective awakening where draconic energy returns to human consciousness to assist in planetary transformation.

The call of the dragons is subtle, but powerful. For those who feel their presence, the answer lies in the inner search, in the development of one's own strength, and in the commitment to truth and balance. Draconic lineages are not just a mystery of the past, but a living legacy, which continues to influence souls who carry within them the essence of these magnificent beings. Awakening to this heritage is recognizing that dragons are not just ancient stories, but timeless forces that continue to act in the evolution of the human spirit.

Chapter 21
Guardians of the Timelines

The connection between dragons and time transcends the linear concept of past, present, and future, revealing a reality where all temporal dimensions coexist. These majestic beings not only master the elements but also exert influence over the tapestry of destiny, ensuring that events follow harmonious patterns within the cosmic flow. In the most ancient spiritual traditions, time dragons are described as guardians of interdimensional passages, sentinels who protect the balance of timelines against interference that could destabilize humanity's evolution. Their presence is felt during critical moments in history, when transitions between eras occur and great changes manifest in the material plane. Those who have a connection with this energy often sense that their existence is not strictly bound to human chronology, as if their souls carry memories of other epochs, ancestral knowledge, and an inexplicable intuition about future events. This connection allows some individuals to access information beyond the present, perceiving cyclical patterns and synchronicities that guide their choices and paths.

The actions of time dragons are subtle yet powerful. They do not control human destiny but ensure that certain evolutionary directions remain intact, preventing external forces from altering the natural course of events. Their presence can be noticed in intensified déjà vu experiences, in revealing dreams that offer glimpses of the future, or even in temporal lapses where the perception of reality momentarily shifts. Some spiritual traditions suggest that these dragons inhabit dimensions where all possibilities exist simultaneously, allowing them to observe and, in some cases, intervene in the paths taken by entire civilizations. In modern accounts of deep meditation and astral projection, there are those who describe encounters with these beings, who appear as immense entities of light and energy, guiding spiritual travelers on their missions and aiding in the understanding of past and future events. This interaction can occur directly, with messages and teachings transmitted clearly, or symbolically, through signs, patterns, and synchronistic encounters that reveal hidden truths.

For those who wish to better understand their connection with time dragons, the path involves developing expanded perception and self-knowledge. Meditation focused on temporal intuition can open doors to hidden memories and awaken awareness of the cycles that govern one's own existence. Observing patterns of repetition in life, recognizing synchronicities, and studying historical records from a new perspective are practices that help strengthen this connection. Furthermore, exploring the Akashic records – an energetic repository where all experiences of existence are stored – can provide valuable insights into the influence of dragons on the timelines. Some traditions believe that these beings are the guardians of this knowledge, allowing access only to those who demonstrate the spiritual maturity to handle the information. By understanding this connection, individuals attuned to this energy begin to see time not as a rigid and immutable line, but as an ocean of interconnected possibilities, where each choice shapes future realities. Thus, time dragons not only observe the unfolding of events but also guide those who are ready to understand and navigate the mysteries of existence with greater clarity and purpose.

Unlike other spiritual forces that operate within the limitations of perceptible reality, time dragons are seen as beings who possess absolute knowledge of temporal weaves and the effects of individual and collective choices. In some traditions, it is believed that they inhabit realms outside of time, where all possibilities coexist, observing and, in some cases, subtly interfering with humanity's destiny. These dragons are said to be responsible for preserving certain events or preventing imbalances that could compromise the integrity of the timelines.

The presence of dragons in mythology is often associated with cyclical events and changes of eras. Some legends speak of dragons that awaken at critical moments in history to restore order or facilitate transitions to new evolutionary phases. This symbolism can be found in ancient texts that describe the rise and fall of civilizations, connecting the draconic awakening to periods of great transformation. In the East, for example, dragons were considered linked to celestial cycles, influencing political and spiritual changes according to astrological and cosmic patterns.

The idea that dragons are guardians of temporal portals also appears in modern accounts of spiritual experiences and astral travels. Some people claim to have encountered these beings in states of deep meditation or projection of consciousness, describing dragons that seem to exist beyond the human concept of time. In these encounters, dragons are often portrayed as immense beings, enveloped in luminous energy, who guide the traveler through visions of the past and future, helping them understand karmic patterns and lessons that need to be integrated.

Some accounts indicate that time dragons act as protectors of universal balance, ensuring that certain events unfold appropriately. There are documented experiences of individuals who perceived inexplicable temporal distortions shortly after feeling a draconic presence. These distortions include time lapses, intensified déjà vu sensations, and the perception of parallel realities coexisting momentarily. For those who study the subject, these occurrences can be interpreted as indications that time dragons are adjusting the temporal weaves to prevent collapses or external interferences that could compromise the natural evolution of a specific timeline.

The relationship between dragons and temporality can also be observed in how certain individuals possess a keen intuition for future events or an inexplicable connection with the past. Some spiritual traditions suggest that those who have a link with time dragons can access memories of other eras or perceive patterns that guide their own journeys. These individuals often report a feeling of being out of sync with ordinary reality, as if they carry fragments of knowledge that do not entirely belong to the present.

Connecting with time dragons requires an expanded perception of reality and a deep respect for the nature of time as an interconnected flow of experiences. Some practices can aid in this connection, such as meditation focused on temporal intuition, where the practitioner concentrates on perceiving the cyclical patterns of their own life and the energies around them. The observation of synchronicities can also be an effective method, as time dragons often communicate their presence through events that seem intentionally organized, guiding the person towards a specific path.

Another way of interacting with this energy is through the exploration of Akashic records, which are described as universal archives where all past, present, and future experiences are stored. Some scholars believe that time dragons act as guardians of these records, allowing access only to those who demonstrate sufficient spiritual maturity to understand and handle the knowledge found there. During practices of reading the Akashic records, there are reports of visions of dragons that appear as sentinels, protecting certain fragments of information and revealing only what is essential for the seeker at that moment.

Time dragons also seem to influence how we perceive destiny and the choices that shape our reality. In some experiences, individuals have reported feeling a strong draconic presence in decisive moments, as if an invisible force were guiding their actions towards an outcome more aligned with their life mission. These subtle influences can manifest as unexpected intuitions, synchronized encounters with people who play fundamental roles in their journey, or the feeling of being carried by an invisible current towards a previously traced path.

The idea that dragons are responsible for protecting the timelines does not mean that they control human destiny absolutely, but rather that they ensure that certain evolutionary directions are not compromised by external interference. Some traditions speak of attempts to manipulate time by forces seeking to alter events for their own benefit, and that dragons act as guardians against these distortions, ensuring that natural order is maintained.

For those who feel a connection with time dragons, understanding this link can be a process of profound transformation. The perception of time as something fluid, rather than linear, allows for a broader understanding of one's own journey and the interconnection between past, present, and future. Working with this energy means learning to recognize the patterns that repeat in life, understanding the cycles of learning, and developing an expanded awareness of the impact of each choice on the flow of existence.

Time dragons represent a mystery that challenges conventional understanding, but their presence can be felt by those who are open to perceiving the signs they leave along the way. They are masters of destiny, guides who help in the crossing of the multiple layers of reality, allowing those who tune into their energy to see beyond the veil of illusion and understand that time is not a limit, but an ocean of infinite possibilities.

Chapter 22
Interdimensional Dragons and the Multiverse

Interdimensional dragons represent one of the most enigmatic and captivating facets of these ancient beings, extending their presence beyond the known boundaries of space and time. Far from being mere mythological figures or guardians of hidden knowledge, these beings operate as cosmic travelers, traversing different planes of existence and interacting with multiple realities simultaneously. Their connection to the multiverse suggests they possess an advanced understanding of the laws governing the structure of reality itself, moving between dimensions and facilitating the energetic exchange between worlds.

For those with spiritual sensitivity, interdimensional dragons reveal themselves as powerful guides, assisting in the awakening of consciousness and the comprehension of the vastness of the cosmos. This contact doesn't occur arbitrarily, but rather when an individual has reached a heightened vibrational state and is prepared to receive information that challenges the conventional perception of reality. Their role transcends simple guardianship of portals or oversight of spiritual planes; they act as teachers, leading seekers to the recognition of their own true, multidimensional nature.

Interaction with these beings often occurs during expanded states of consciousness, such as lucid dreams, astral projections, and deep meditations. Accounts of encounters with interdimensional dragons describe environments that defy the laws of traditional physics: vast crystal cities suspended in the void, oceans of fluid energy, and colossal temples where ancient symbols glow with an inner light. In these spaces, the linear perception of time ceases to exist, allowing the traveler to simultaneously experience past, present, and future events.

Some spiritual traditions suggest that these dragons guard secrets about the structure of the multiverse, protecting knowledge that can only be accessed by those who demonstrate spiritual maturity and responsibility. This connection can result in powerful energetic activations, awakening latent abilities within the individual, such as clairvoyance, expanded intuition, and an instinctive understanding of the cosmic patterns that govern existence. These manifestations indicate that interdimensional dragons not only observe parallel realities but also influence the spiritual evolution of those ready to transcend the limitations of the physical world.

To establish conscious contact with interdimensional dragons, it's essential to expand perception beyond the limits of conventional thought. Techniques such as visualizing portals, utilizing specific vibrational frequencies, and exploring the Akashic records are paths that allow one to adjust their consciousness to perceive their presence. Furthermore, some cultures believe that certain power spots, such as sacred mountains and megalithic formations, function as intersection points between dimensions, facilitating access to these beings.

Reports of experiences in high-energy locations describe phenomena such as luminous apparitions in the form of dragons, abrupt temperature variations, and intense electrical discharges in the environment, indicating that these beings actively interact with those who demonstrate respect and a genuine intention to learn. However, their communication doesn't always occur verbally or linearly; they often transmit teachings through symbols, recurring patterns, and insights that gradually unfold within the seeker's consciousness.

Thus, the connection with interdimensional dragons is not just a journey of discovery of the universe, but also a profound process of self-discovery and transformation, in which the individual learns to navigate the hidden layers of existence and understand their own multidimensional essence.

The multiverse theory proposes that our reality is not unique, but rather one among infinite versions of existence, where different possibilities and variations of matter, time, and consciousness coexist simultaneously. In this context, dragons would be cosmic travelers capable of manifesting in various realities, interacting with those who possess the sensitivity necessary to perceive their presence. Some traditions claim that dragons operate as guardians of these interdimensional portals, ensuring that certain knowledge and energies are not accessed without proper preparation.

Reports of spiritual contacts with dragons suggest that their presence is often perceived in altered states of consciousness, such as lucid dreams, deep meditations, and experiences of astral projection. Some people claim to have encountered dragons in landscapes that do not correspond to the physical world, describing vast crystal cities, oceans suspended in the air, and luminous temples that seem to exist beyond human comprehension. These descriptions reinforce the idea that dragons are not confined to our dimension, but that they operate in realms beyond time and space, where the laws of physics and logic are different from those we know.

The influence of these beings on the expansion of human consciousness can be observed in the way they interact with those who seek them. Some spiritual traditions teach that interdimensional dragons are responsible for awakening ancestral memories and activating latent capacities in the human spirit. This means that their contact does not occur only as a visual or symbolic experience, but also as an energetic activation that allows the individual to access information and abilities that were dormant. This activation can manifest as an increase in intuition, a greater facility to perceive subtle patterns in reality, or even the ability to access higher states of consciousness with more clarity.

Connecting with interdimensional dragons requires an appropriate mental and vibrational state.

Those who attempt to establish this contact must first expand their perception beyond the limits of conventional reality. Techniques such as guided meditation, the use of specific sound frequencies, and the practice of astral projection are effective ways to align the mind and spirit with these beings. Some traditions teach that visualizing portals or ancient symbols can serve as a tuning mechanism, allowing the individual to adjust their frequency to perceive the dragons in their interdimensional form.

In addition to individual experiences, there are reports of groups that have performed rituals and ceremonies in places of high energy, such as sacred mountains, untouched forests, or ancient stone circles, and who have felt the draconic presence intensely. In some cases, members of these groups described seeing figures of light in the form of dragons appearing in the sky or felt waves of heat and electricity running through the environment. These manifestations were interpreted as signs that interdimensional dragons were communicating, responding to the call of those who seek to understand them.

Interpreting the messages left by these dragons can be a challenge, as their forms of communication do not always follow human patterns. In many accounts, interactions occur through symbolic images, intensified emotions, or an instantaneous understanding of concepts that previously seemed abstract. Some people claim that, after an experience with interdimensional dragons, they began to see reality differently, as if they had received a new perspective on their own existence and the structure of the universe.

The existence of interdimensional dragons suggests that there is much more to be understood about the nature of reality than the conventional view allows. If these beings really do travel between different planes, it would indicate that the universe operates with more complex rules than we imagine. For those who feel the call to explore this connection, the key lies in expanding consciousness and the willingness to question the limits of human perception.

The dragons of the multiverse are not only guardians of portals or entities of higher planes, but also teachers who challenge those who seek them to overcome their own limitations. Their role is not to provide ready-made answers, but to instigate the search for knowledge and awakening. For those who connect with this energy, the journey is not just about understanding the dragons, but about understanding themselves and the vastness of existence that surrounds them.

Chapter 23
Dragons in the New Age

Humanity is living through a time of profound transition, where old structures are dissolving and a new consciousness is beginning to emerge. This awakening isn't just happening on a social and technological level, but primarily in the spiritual realm, where ancestral forces are returning to guide this transformative process. Among these forces, draconic energy is resurfacing with intensity, not as legendary creatures dominating the skies, but as a subtle and powerful presence influencing the expansion of human perception. Dragons have always been symbols of wisdom, strength, and renewal, and their influence in the New Age is linked to the awakening of a knowledge that has been dormant for centuries. This return represents more than a cultural or mythological revival; it's about reactivating ancient codes that help humanity overcome the limitations of a materialistic worldview and reconnect with the cosmic principles that govern existence. Many who feel this connection describe an inner calling, an urgency to seek understanding and growth, as if they are awakening to a greater mission aligned with the collective evolution of the planet.

The role of dragons in this new cycle is directly related to accelerating the process of spiritual ascension. As guardians of hidden knowledge, they offer guidance to those who are ready to access a broader reality, where consciousness is no longer restricted to what the physical senses can perceive. This contact can occur through vivid dreams, deep meditative experiences, and intuitions that arise as transformative insights. Some spiritual traditions suggest that dragons are guardians of interdimensional portals, allowing individuals with certain vibrational frequencies to receive information that was previously inaccessible. Draconic energy, therefore, acts as a catalyst for the expansion of perception, helping humanity to transcend old paradigms based on fear, separation, and limitation. However, this connection doesn't happen passively; it requires commitment, discipline, and a genuine willingness to integrate this knowledge into everyday life. Dragons don't impose their teachings, but offer them to those who demonstrate maturity and responsibility to handle them.

As humanity advances in this transition process, the return of draconic energy becomes increasingly evident. The growing interest in spirituality, the search for balance between science and consciousness, and the need to restore respect for nature are signs that this influence is intensifying. Working in harmony with this energy means accepting transformation as an essential part of the journey and developing the courage to break patterns that no longer serve personal and collective growth. The dragons of the New Age don't appear to protect or guide passively, but to challenge and strengthen those who are ready to assume their true role in the planet's evolution. Their presence is not a mere remnant of ancient mythologies, but an active force that drives human awakening, encouraging each individual to recognize their own power and their unbreakable connection with the universe. Those who respond to the call of the dragons understand that the journey is not about seeking external answers, but about accessing inner wisdom and taking responsibility for their own evolution.

The connection of dragons to this transition process is perceived by those who feel profound internal changes, such as a calling to a greater mission, a need to realign their lives with a higher purpose, or a growing awareness of the interconnectedness of all things. Dragons have always been symbols of transformation, and their energy is present in times of great change, aiding in the destruction of what no longer serves and the construction of something new. Their influence manifests both on an individual and collective level, guiding those who are ready to access this new consciousness and contributing to the global awakening.

The return of draconic energy is not random. Many scholars of spirituality believe that dragons are guardians of ancient codes, information that was hidden until humanity was ready to understand it again. This knowledge, which may be stored in sacred places, in the Earth's energy structure, or even in the spiritual DNA of certain lineages, begins to gradually reveal itself as more people awaken to this reality. Resonance with this energy can be perceived in dreams, intuitions, synchronous manifestations, and intense meditative experiences, where individuals report feeling the draconic presence in an unmistakable way.

The role of dragons in the New Age seems to be that of guides and protectors of this process of ascension of consciousness. In various cultures, dragons have been portrayed as masters of hidden wisdom, those who guard the deepest secrets of existence and who only reveal this knowledge to those who demonstrate sufficient spiritual maturity to receive it. This archetype now resurfaces with force, showing that humanity is at a decisive moment, where it can choose to remain trapped in old patterns of fear and separation or open itself to a new level of understanding and evolution.

Working in tune with this energy means being willing to break down internal and external barriers, abandon limiting beliefs, and open oneself to the expansion of perception. Dragons don't offer easy answers or smooth paths; they challenge those who seek them to take responsibility for their own journey, to develop inner strength, and to act with courage in the face of the changes that are necessary. This means that, to access this connection consciously, one must be willing to grow, face challenges, and integrate draconic wisdom into everyday life.

Humanity can learn much from dragons if it knows how to listen to their teachings. In a world where the balance between technology and spirituality has become one of the greatest challenges, draconic energy can act as a bridge between these two aspects, teaching the importance of discernment, responsibility, and respect for the natural flow of existence. True power lies not in the imposition of force, but in mastery over oneself, and this is one of the fundamental lessons that dragons teach to those who are ready to understand their essence.

The signs of the return of the dragons can already be observed in different areas. The growing interest in spiritual practices that involve connection with ancestral forces, the awakening of intuitive abilities in many people, and the collective feeling that something is changing are indications that we are approaching a new cycle. There are reports of individuals who claim to feel the draconic presence at unexpected moments, as an energy that protects and guides them, and there are those who perceive repetitive patterns, symbols, and messages that seem to indicate a greater calling.

The future of humanity seems to be intertwined with this reconnection. As more people awaken to the reality beyond the visible, contact with dragons becomes more accessible, not as a fantastical experience, but as a reunion with an ancient force that has always been present, waiting for the right moment to manifest again. This return does not mean that dragons will take an active role in physical life, but rather that their energetic presence will be increasingly perceived, influencing those who are attuned to their frequency.

The New Age is not just about external changes, but primarily about a profound internal transformation, where human consciousness expands to understand reality in a broader and more integrated way. Dragons, as archetypes of primordial wisdom and cosmic power, play an essential role in this process, helping to remove the veils of illusion and allowing humanity to perceive its true nature. Those who listen to the call of the dragons have already begun to feel this change and know that the path ahead requires commitment, courage, and authenticity.

The return of draconic energy is not just a symbolic event, but a milestone in the evolution of planetary consciousness. For those who wish to align themselves with this energy, the first step is to open themselves to transformation, accept the challenge of self-knowledge, and seek to live in harmony with the principles that dragons represent: truth, strength, balance, and respect for life in all its forms. The future may be uncertain, but for those who walk alongside the dragons, the journey will always be an adventure towards the awakening of the true essence of being.

Chapter 24
Meditations with Dragons

Dragon meditation is a profound practice that allows one to access the energy of these ancestral entities and interact directly with their wisdom. These beings don't manifest casually or arbitrarily; their presence is felt by those who are prepared to receive their teachings and integrate their power into a process of spiritual evolution. Establishing this connection requires more than simply sitting down and seeking a superficial contact – it demands aligning mind, body, and spirit, raising one's personal vibration to a state of genuine receptivity. Dragons represent archetypes of transformation and inner power, and their presence in meditation can bring impactful revelations, unlock dormant potential, and provoke profound shifts in one's perception of reality. For those who feel the call of these beings, meditation not only strengthens the bond with their energy but also opens pathways to a broader understanding of one's own spiritual journey.

The first step towards this connection is to create a conducive environment, where the practitioner can feel safe and at peace, far from distractions. The posture should be comfortable, allowing the breath to flow freely and the body to remain relaxed. Conscious breathing is fundamental in this process, as it helps to tune the mind to higher frequencies, opening the energy field to the dragon's presence. Many practitioners report that the connection with dragons occurs more intensely when there is a clear intention, expressed with respect and sincerity. Visualizing a portal of light, an ancient temple, or a mystical landscape can facilitate this encounter, as these elements symbolize passages to dimensions where dragons reside. Some people perceive their presence as a warm and vibrant energy, while others see vivid images of these imposing beings. Regardless of how they manifest, dragons communicate in subtle ways, using symbols, emotions, and insights that are revealed progressively.

As the practitioner deepens their connection, they may begin to receive messages, guidance, or sensations that indicate the dragon's presence in their daily life. Some experiences involve symbolic dreams, where dragons appear as guides or protectors, conveying teachings through metaphors and challenges. Others report noticeable changes in their personal energy, becoming more confident, determined, and intuitive after establishing this bond. The continuous practice of dragon meditation strengthens this relationship, allowing the wisdom of these beings to be gradually assimilated and applied in daily life. Contact with this energy requires commitment and a sincere desire for spiritual growth, as dragons do not offer easy answers – they challenge, transform, and empower those who are ready to tread a path of self-discovery and evolution. Thus, this practice is not merely a means of establishing spiritual contact, but a journey to access dormant inner strengths and integrate the dragon's power and wisdom into one's very essence.

The importance of meditation in this process lies in the energetic alignment it provides. Dragons are beings that vibrate at a high frequency, and to perceive them consciously, the practitioner needs to raise their own vibration. This means that the mind must be free from agitation, and the body relaxed, so that the connection can occur fluidly. Dragon energy cannot be invoked forcibly or anxiously; patience and respect are needed, as these beings do not respond to calls that are not aligned with the genuine intention of learning and evolution.

There are different methods for meditating and feeling the dragon's presence. One of the most common is guided meditation, where the practitioner visualizes a specific environment and opens themselves to the experience. This method is particularly useful for those who have not yet developed a keen energetic sensitivity, as visualization helps create a mental space conducive to the dragons' manifestation. Another technique involves the use of mantras or specific sounds that resonate with the energy of dragons, allowing the practitioner to tune their frequency to theirs. Breathing also plays a fundamental role, as controlling the flow of air within the body helps to calm the mind and stabilize personal energy.

Visualization is one of the most important aspects of dragon meditation. To begin this practice, it is recommended that the practitioner find a quiet place, where they will not be interrupted. Sitting or lying down, they should close their eyes and begin to imagine a vast and powerful landscape, such as an ancient mountain, a dense forest, or an endless ocean. This setting should be vividly constructed, allowing all the details to be felt, from the temperature of the environment to the surrounding sounds. After establishing this setting, the practitioner should focus their intention on encountering their dragon. One can imagine a bright light appearing on the horizon, a shadow crossing the sky, or even an energy that manifests as warmth and vibration around the body.

The moment of encounter is unique for each person. Some report seeing a huge dragon approaching, while others only feel its presence without a defined image. Some people hear words or feel deep emotions that seem not to come from themselves, as if the dragon were transmitting a teaching directly to their consciousness. There are those who perceive symbols, patterns, or colors that, later, they discover have specific meanings related to their spiritual journey. Regardless of how the dragon manifests, the most important thing is to trust the experience and not try to control it rationally.

During meditation, it is common for the practitioner to experience intense physical sensations. Some people report a sudden warmth, as if an inner flame were lit within them, while others feel chills or a slight pressure in the center of the forehead, indicating the activation of the third eye. There are also reports of a feeling of expansion, as if consciousness were moving beyond the limits of the physical body. These experiences may vary, but they all indicate that the connection is being established and that the dragon energy is acting on the practitioner's vibrational field.

Interpreting these experiences can be a challenge, especially for those who are starting. The most important thing is to observe how the energy manifests in daily life after meditation. Often, dragons send messages through dreams, synchronicities, or sudden insights that help the practitioner understand hidden aspects of their own journey. Some people perceive changes in their personality, feeling more secure, determined, and aligned with their purpose. Others begin to notice external signs, such as images of dragons repeatedly appearing in different contexts, indicating that the connection has been established and that the dragons are communicating symbolically.

To deepen this practice over time, it is essential to maintain a consistent meditation routine. The more the practitioner dedicates themselves to this process, the easier it becomes to access the dragon energy and interpret its teachings. In addition, it can be helpful to record experiences in a journal, noting details of visions, emotions, and messages received. Over time, patterns may emerge, revealing a line of learning that the dragons are progressively guiding.

Connecting with dragons through meditation is not something that develops instantly, but rather a gradual process that requires dedication and respect. These beings do not manifest for those who seek them out of superficial curiosity or a desire for power, but for those who are genuinely committed to their own spiritual evolution. The practitioner must be willing to accept the challenges and transformations that this connection can bring, as dragons not only teach but also test those who approach their energy.

For those who feel the call of the dragons, meditation is the safest and most effective way to establish a real bond with these beings. The practice not only allows their presence to be perceived, but also creates a relationship of mutual trust, where the practitioner learns to recognize the signs and integrate the dragon's wisdom into their daily life. Those who persist on this journey discover that dragons are not just symbols of strength and protection, but true spiritual masters who can guide the soul to higher levels of consciousness and understanding.

Chapter 25
Invocations and Energy Circles

Connecting with dragons through invocations and energy circles represents a path of profound spiritual deepening, where the practitioner opens themselves to the presence and wisdom of these ancestral forces. Unlike a casual call, an invocation is a respectful invitation, a request for guidance and learning, rooted in humility and a genuine intention for growth. Dragons are not entities that respond to mere curiosity or superficial desires; they manifest to those who demonstrate commitment and spiritual maturity. Thus, preparation for this contact is essential, requiring an energetic alignment that allows their presence to be perceived clearly and safely. This process involves purifying the environment, raising one's personal vibration, and creating a sacred space where energy can flow without blockage. Those who wish to tread this path must understand that dragons act as guardians and teachers, testing the practitioner's willingness to face internal challenges and evolve spiritually.

Creating an energy circle is one of the most effective methods for establishing a deep and protected connection with dragons. This circle can be drawn physically, using crystals, candles, or sacred symbols, or energetically, through visualization and intention. The structure of this sacred space serves as a portal that facilitates communication with dragons, while simultaneously protecting the practitioner from external influences that might interfere with the experience. During the invocation, words of power can be used to tune the energetic frequency to the draconic presence. Some traditions teach that each dragon has a unique vibrational name, discovered through meditative practice or intuitive revelations. Expressing this call authentically and respectfully strengthens the connection, allowing energy to flow freely and the signs of the dragons' presence to become perceptible. The experience can manifest in various ways – a sensation of intense heat, a subtle wind in the environment, or even vivid images in the mind – indicating that contact has been successfully established.

After the invocation, gratitude plays a fundamental role in maintaining this spiritual relationship. Thanking the dragons for their presence, regardless of the intensity of the experience, demonstrates respect and strengthens the bond with these forces. The closing of the circle should be done with awareness, dissipating the generated energy in a balanced and intentional way. For those who wish to deepen this practice, keeping a journal of experiences can be useful for recording perceptions, messages received, and recurring patterns that emerge over time. As the connection becomes stronger, the practitioner begins to integrate the wisdom of the dragons into their life, becoming more intuitive, resilient, and aligned with their true essence. The journey with dragons is not just an exercise in invocation, but a path of self-discovery and transformation, where those who prove themselves worthy receive not only protection and knowledge, but also the challenge to grow and expand their consciousness beyond the limits of conventional reality.

Preparation for an invocation is one of the most crucial aspects of the process. The space where the ritual will be performed must be energetically clean, as dragons respond to environments where energy flows without blockages or interference. Cleansing can be done with incense, herbs, or crystals that help remove any disharmonious vibrations. The choice of location is also fundamental, preferably an environment where the practitioner can concentrate without interruptions. Some prefer to perform this practice outdoors, especially in natural locations that have a strong presence of the elements, such as mountains, forests, or by rivers and oceans.

Creating a draconic energy circle strengthens the connection and protects the ritual space. The circle can be drawn physically, using stones, candles, or specific symbols, or energetically, through visualization. When drawing the circle, the practitioner can imagine a ring of fire, water, wind, or golden light around them, symbolizing the presence of the dragons and the activation of the energy field. Within this space, the mind and heart must be in tune with the intention of the ritual, as dragons do not respond to empty requests or those motivated by selfish interests.

Words of power can be used to facilitate the connection. Some traditions teach that each dragon has a vibrational name, a sound that resonates with its essence and can be used to call it respectfully. These names are not revealed lightly and are often discovered through meditative experiences or dreams. Additionally, invocation phrases can be created intuitively, expressing the intention of connection and learning. An example of an invocation might be something like: "Great ancestral guardians, dragons of time and the elements, I call upon you with respect and humility. If it is within my deserving journey, may your wisdom be revealed and your energy guide me."

The use of symbols also strengthens the invocation. Some traditions use specific sigils, created to represent the draconic presence and serve as portals for their energy. These symbols can be drawn on the ground, on parchment, or even visualized in the mind. Crystals such as obsidian, smoky quartz, and citrine are known for their affinity with dragons and can be placed within the circle to anchor the energy. Other elements, such as colored candles representing the different aspects of dragons – fire, water, earth, and air – can be used to reinforce the presence of the elements in the ritual.

Working with draconic energy requires caution and ethics. These beings possess an intense vibration and do not tolerate manipulation or irresponsible attempts at invocation. A common mistake among beginners is trying to force contact without proper preparation or respect, which can result in an uncomfortable experience or a total disconnection. Dragons are not passive entities; they test those who call upon them and may withdraw if they perceive that the practitioner is not prepared to handle their energy. Therefore, it is essential that the intention of the invocation is clear, respectful, and aligned with the purpose of learning and spiritual growth.

During the ritual, it is common for certain sensations to manifest. Some people report a sudden increase in body temperature, indicating the presence of a fire dragon, while others feel a light breeze around the circle, signaling the influence of an air dragon. There are also those who perceive a weight on their shoulders or a wave of deep calm, suggesting that the connection has been established. Subtle sounds, such as crackling in the environment or a distant echo, can be interpreted as signs that the dragons are attentive to the invocation.

After the invocation, it is essential to demonstrate gratitude for the presence of the dragons, regardless of whether there has been a clear manifestation or not. The closing of the ritual should be done respectfully, dismantling the circle with intention and thanking for the opportunity of connection. The practitioner can leave a symbolic offering, such as a crystal, a candle, or even a sincere thought of recognition for the experience lived.

The practice of invocation and draconic energy circles should not be seen as an isolated event, but as a path of continuous learning. The more a practitioner dedicates themselves to this journey, the more attuned they become to the energy of the dragons and the clearer their communication with them becomes. Those who persist on this path not only develop a deep connection with these beings, but also transform their own essence, becoming stronger, wiser, and aligned with the primordial forces of the universe.

Chapter 26
How to Honor the Dragons

Dragons are ancestral forces that transcend mythology and symbolism, manifesting as guardians of primordial knowledge and power. Their essence resonates across diverse cultures throughout history, revered not merely as legendary creatures, but as spiritual entities representing fundamental elements of existence. Unlike spiritual beings accessible through passive devotion, dragons demand a conscious and respectful approach, where the connection is built upon pillars of honor, commitment, and a deep understanding of their nature. Each encounter with these forces requires authenticity, for their presence is not revealed to those seeking only personal gain, but to those who demonstrate dedication and a genuine intention to comprehend their energy.

The act of honoring dragons goes beyond simple ritualistic practice; it's about an inner alignment with the values these beings represent. Courage, wisdom, loyalty, and transformation are essential aspects of this relationship, and any attempt to connect with dragons without embodying these qualities will result in a superficial or even non-existent interaction. They are not impressed by empty gestures or promises made without conviction. On the contrary, they carefully observe the practitioner's conduct over time, assessing whether their actions are truly aligned with the draconic essence. This evaluation process should not be seen as an obstacle, but as an invitation to self-awareness and spiritual refinement.

Reverence for dragons involves both symbolic offerings and concrete actions in daily life. Respect for oneself and the natural cycles, the constant pursuit of self-improvement, and the defense of what is sacred are practical manifestations of this commitment. The elements offered in rituals should reflect more than a desire to please these entities; they must carry the sincere intention of establishing a bond based on reciprocity. Thus, true homage is not limited to an altar or a one-time gesture, but is manifested in the way the practitioner conducts their journey, cultivating discipline, resilience, and responsibility in the face of the knowledge they seek to access.

The nature of the offerings may vary depending on the type of dragon and the intention of the ritual. For fire dragons, elements that represent the sacred flame are appropriate, such as red or gold candles, incense of strong resins like myrrh and frankincense, and even small volcanic rocks left on outdoor altars. These dragons appreciate actions that demonstrate courage and transformation, so burning papers containing fears or negative patterns to be transmuted can be a powerful symbolic offering.

Water dragons, in turn, are linked to emotional flow and intuition, preferring offerings that carry the essence of fluidity and purity. Natural water sources, such as streams, waterfalls, and lakes, are ideal places to honor them. Crystals energized in running water, bowls of water consecrated with herbs like chamomile or lavender, or even shells and pearls can be left as symbols of respect. Additionally, practicing emotional self-care and inner purification are ways to honor these dragons, as they value balance and the natural flow of life.

For earth dragons, solid and grounded elements are more appropriate. Rocks from sacred places, seeds, grains, and crystals like black tourmaline or jasper are good options. Planting a tree or caring for a natural space can be seen as a living offering, demonstrating the practitioner's commitment to the preservation of the Earth, a fundamental value for these dragons. These offerings need not be left on physical altars, but rather integrated into one's routine in a conscious way, as a continuous act of respect for the planet and the forces that sustain it.

Air dragons are interdimensional messengers and appreciate offerings that involve sound, movement, and clear mental intention. Mantras, music played in their honor, symbolic feathers, or even the practice of conscious breathing are ways to offer something meaningful to these dragons. The use of light incense, such as sandalwood and lavender, or of bells and Tibetan singing bowls can facilitate attunement with their energy. Meditating in high places, such as mountains or terraces, where the wind circulates freely, is a symbolic way of acknowledging their presence and demonstrating reverence.

Rituals of honor and gratitude to the dragons can be simple, but they must always be performed with truth and respect. Creating a small altar, whether in the physical or mental environment, and dedicating a few moments to express recognition can be a first step. Offerings can be accompanied by spontaneous words or ritual phrases that express gratitude, such as: "I am grateful for your presence and the wisdom shared. May my journey continue in tune with the draconic energy, and may I honor this connection with awareness and truth."

The spiritual significance of offerings lies in the intention and energy invested in them. When done sincerely, these practices create a vibrational link between the practitioner and the dragons, allowing their energy to manifest more clearly and presently. More than material objects, dragons value attitudes aligned with their essence, such as the pursuit of knowledge, overcoming challenges, and protecting what is sacred.

Practitioners who have incorporated the habit of making offerings and demonstrations of respect often report significant changes in their spiritual journeys. Some notice an increase in intuition, feeling the dragons guiding them through dreams, synchronicities, and profound insights. Others report a constant sense of protection and inner strength, as if they were accompanied by an invisible, yet powerful presence. There are also those who notice a greater flow of opportunities and learning, as if the connection with the dragons were aligning their path with a greater purpose.

Honoring dragons does not mean only performing occasional rituals, but rather living according to principles that resonate with their energy. Demonstrating loyalty, courage, and respect for knowledge are attitudes that strengthen this connection more than any physical offering. Dragons are beings that observe the essence of individuals, and those who demonstrate commitment to their own spiritual growth naturally become more receptive to their presence.

The relationship with dragons is a two-way street, where trust and genuine exchange are the pillars that sustain this interaction. For those who wish to deepen this bond, the key lies in authenticity. More than symbolic gestures, dragons value the truth of the heart and the coherence between words and actions. By honoring them sincerely, the practitioner not only strengthens their connection with these beings, but also aligns themselves with an energy of power and wisdom that can transform their journey in a profound and lasting way.

Chapter 27
Messages from the Unconscious

The realm of dreams is a vast and mysterious territory, where the unconscious communicates through symbols, archetypes, and intense experiences that transcend the logic of our waking state. In this realm, the human mind disconnects from rational barriers and opens itself to dimensions where primordial forces can manifest. Among these forces, dragons emerge as figures of profound significance, representing challenges, protection, power, and wisdom. Their presence in dreams is not random; on the contrary, it reflects internal aspects of the dreamer, conveying messages that can aid in the process of self-discovery and personal transformation. Interaction with dragons in the oneiric world can be a call to awaken a dormant inner strength, confront hidden fears, or even an invitation to establish a deeper spiritual connection with these entities.

The way dragons appear in dreams varies according to the emotional state and life circumstances of each individual. For some, they appear as imposing creatures, challenging the dreamer to face their own limits and overcome internal obstacles. For others, they manifest as allies or guides, offering protection and guidance in times of uncertainty. Interpreting these appearances requires sensitivity and attention to the details of the dream, as each element—color, behavior, environment, and emotions involved—carries a meaning that can reveal hidden messages. For example, a dragon that rises before the dreamer in a threatening manner may represent a repressed fear that needs to be faced, while a serene dragon that allows approach may symbolize the discovery of a new potential or a developing spiritual connection.

Beyond individual symbolism, dreams with dragons can be authentic spiritual experiences, in which the dreamer's consciousness accesses subtle planes of existence. Some esoteric traditions believe that dragons inhabit ethereal realms and that, during sleep, it is possible to establish direct contact with these entities. In these cases, the dream is distinguished by its intensity and clarity, leaving a deep impression upon awakening. Dreams of this type are generally accompanied by vivid sensations, direct messages, and an atmosphere of realism that distinguishes them from mere creations of the subconscious mind. For those who wish to better understand these experiences, keeping a dream journal and practicing induction techniques, such as meditation before sleep or the use of crystals that promote dream recall, can be a way to deepen this connection and decipher the teachings that dragons have to offer.

The symbolic meaning of dragons in dreams is linked to transformation, power, and connection with primordial forces. In many cultures, the dragon represents internal challenges that need to be overcome, primordial instincts that must be integrated, or even the need to face personal fears and limitations. When a dragon appears in the dream world, it may be bringing to the surface repressed aspects of the psyche, such as unexpressed anger, unclaimed courage, or a call to expand consciousness. On the other hand, depending on the context of the dream, a dragon can represent protection, ancestral wisdom, or the presence of a spiritual guide assisting in the journey of self-discovery.

Dragons can also act as true guides within the dream world, aiding in the understanding of mysteries and providing teachings that would not be easily accessible in the waking state. Some esoteric traditions suggest that certain souls have ancient connections with these beings and, during sleep, can receive direct instructions about their life mission, spiritual paths, or even unknown aspects of reality. There are reports of dreamers who, upon encountering a dragon in dreams, received visions of future events, information about their personal development, or insights into issues that afflicted them.

Differentiating a purely symbolic dream from a real spiritual experience with dragons can be challenging, but there are some characteristics that help in this distinction. Ordinary dreams tend to be fragmented, with disconnected elements and an irregular flow of events. Spiritual experiences with dragons, however, are usually incredibly vivid, with a clarity that transcends the usual logic of dreams. Often, dreamers report a sense of real presence, as if they were facing an independent consciousness that interacts autonomously.

In addition, these dreams frequently leave a lasting emotional impact, accompanied by a feeling of profound learning or spiritual awakening.

For those who wish to interpret and record their dreams with dragons, keeping a dream journal is an essential practice. As soon as you wake up, the dreamer should write down all possible details of the experience, including colors, sensations, interactions, and emotions involved. Each element of the dream can carry a hidden meaning, and over time, patterns may emerge, revealing recurring messages or specific themes that the dragons are trying to communicate. The analysis of these dreams can be done intuitively, connecting with the feeling that each image awakens, or using symbolic and mythological references for a more in-depth interpretation.

In addition to recording, lucid dream induction techniques can be used to facilitate conscious contact with dragons in the oneiric world. Methods such as practicing mindfulness during the day, using affirmations before sleep, and repeating the intention to meet a dragon in the dream can increase the chances of a meaningful encounter. Some practitioners also use crystals such as amethyst or lapis lazuli under the pillow, as they are known to amplify the connection with the dream plane and facilitate spiritual experiences.

Reports from people who have had profound encounters with dragons in dreams suggest that these experiences can cause significant changes in waking life. Some describe that, after dreaming of a dragon, they began to feel more confidence and inner strength, as if they had received an energetic boost to overcome challenges. Others report that the dragons provided enigmatic messages that, when deciphered, helped to clarify important aspects of their lives. There are also those who claim to have seen dragons in multiple dreams over the years, each time bringing new revelations, as if a gradual learning process were taking place.

Dragons in dreams are not just figures of fantasy or random elements of the subconscious, but rather powerful manifestations of forces that operate beyond what we can rationally comprehend. For those who feel the call of these beings, paying attention to dreams can be one of the most direct paths to establishing a meaningful connection. The unconscious speaks through symbols, and dragons, when they appear, bring with them messages that can transform the perception of reality and expand consciousness to new dimensions of knowledge and spiritual awakening.

Chapter 28
Personal Development

Personal development, fueled by the energy of dragons, is an intense and transformative journey, one where an individual's inner strength is awakened and refined. This connection isn't passive; dragons aren't entities that offer comfort without effort. On the contrary, they challenge those who seek their presence, demanding commitment, courage, and the willingness to confront truths that are often hidden. The draconic influence not only strengthens personality and determination but also guides the practitioner in discovering their true potential, showing that real evolution occurs when one is willing to face challenges and transcend self-imposed limits.

The energy of dragons acts as a catalyst for profound change, helping to transform insecurities into self-confidence and fears into opportunities for growth. Many who come into contact with this force report a heightened sense of purpose and an increased ability to make decisions with greater conviction. This is because dragons do not tolerate hesitation when it comes to following one's own path. They teach that each person is responsible for forging their own journey and that the power to shape reality lies within. However, this power isn't freely given; it must be claimed through authenticity and continuous effort. With each obstacle overcome, the individual becomes stronger, more self-aware, and more aligned with their true essence.

Commitment to personal development under the guidance of dragons isn't limited to specific moments of introspection or spiritual practice. It's about a shift in how one lives and interacts with the world. Draconic energy manifests in both small and large daily choices: in how we face challenges, how we stand up in the face of adversity, and in the willingness to persist even when the path seems uncertain. Incorporating draconic principles – courage, authenticity, wisdom, and responsibility – means adopting an attitude of constant learning and growth. Those who accept this journey find that dragons not only inspire transformation but also serve as guides to a fuller life, one aligned with the true potential of being.

The influence of dragons on personal growth can be perceived in various ways. One of the most striking aspects is the strengthening of self-confidence. Many who initiate this connection report a profound transformation in their approach to life, feeling more secure in expressing their truth, making important decisions, and taking responsibility for their journey. This is because dragons teach that true strength comes from within, and that no one can fully master their reality without first mastering themselves. Draconic energy inspires self-reliance and the courage to walk unknown paths, trusting in one's own intuition and inner power.

Another significant impact of this connection is the development of emotional and mental resilience. Dragons often challenge those who seek them, confronting them with their shadows and limitations. This process can be intense, as it requires facing insecurities, fears, and limiting beliefs head-on. However, those who accept this challenge discover that they are much stronger than they imagined. This inner strength doesn't come from denial or repression, but from the acceptance and integration of one's own weaknesses as part of the growth process. Just as a dragon flies freely through storms without faltering, the individual learns to navigate turbulent moments in life with wisdom and balance.

Incorporating the teachings of dragons into daily life requires practice and commitment. The first step is to recognize the presence of this energy and open oneself to its lessons. This can be done through meditation, where the practitioner connects with the essence of dragons and allows their strength to manifest internally. Another way to apply these teachings is through concrete actions that reflect draconic values, such as honesty, courage, and respect for one's own truth. Every choice made with integrity strengthens this connection and expands the positive influence of dragons on the personal journey.

The presence of dragons can also be invoked in moments of decision-making. In situations where doubt or fear arise, one can visualize a dragon by their side, as a guardian of clarity and determination. This simple practice can bring a sense of security and encouragement, allowing the person to make decisions that are more aligned with their purpose. Furthermore, working with the energy of dragons in specific challenges – such as public speaking, facing a personal obstacle, or starting a new project – can be a powerful way to integrate their strength into everyday life.

Many people who have connected with dragons report profound changes in their lives. Some have experienced a significant increase in courage and boldness, allowing themselves to explore new paths without fear of failure. Others have found that their intuition has become sharper, making it easier to understand signs and messages from the universe. There are also those who have developed a clearer sense of purpose, feeling guided by a greater force in their journey. These transformations do not occur instantaneously, but rather as a continuous process of maturation and self-discovery, where each step taken further strengthens the connection with this ancestral energy.

Dragons act as teachers and catalysts of human evolution because they challenge stagnation and propel growth. Unlike spiritual guides who offer comfort and protection, dragons teach through overcoming, placing the individual before trials that lead them to become stronger. Their role is not to carry anyone on their shoulders, but to teach them how to create their own wings and fly independently. This approach may seem rigorous to some, but it is precisely this demand that makes the connection with dragons so transformative.

Working with dragons is a commitment to walking with integrity, strength, and purpose. It is a call to those who do not fear change and who are ready to access their true potential. Those who accept this call discover that dragons are not just myths or distant archetypes, but living forces that act in the development of the soul, guiding each one towards a more authentic and powerful existence.

Chapter 29
How to Sense the Presence of Dragons

The presence of dragons in the spiritual realm doesn't reveal itself in obvious or direct ways. Instead, it manifests through subtle signs and experiences that defy everyday logic. These beings, bearers of an ancient and powerful energy, make themselves known to those who are open to perceiving their influence – whether through vivid dreams, sudden intuitions, or synchronicities that become impossible to ignore. More than mere mythological figures or archetypes of the collective unconscious, dragons represent a living force that resonates with those seeking growth, courage, and a deeper connection with the mysteries of the universe. Sensing their presence doesn't depend on blind faith, but on a heightened sensitivity and a willingness to recognize patterns and messages that may be hidden in daily experiences.

For those who feel called by this energy, the first indications of draconic presence often arise spontaneously. A sudden interest in dragon symbols, an inexplicable attraction to stories or representations of these beings, and even changes in the way one perceives the surrounding environment are some of the most common signs. Some people report an increase in inner strength, as if an invisible presence is urging them to face challenges with more determination. Others experience moments of intense clarity, as if receiving advice or guidance from a source that transcends the rational mind. Physical sensations, such as a sudden warmth in the body, a shiver that cannot be explained, or even a subtle variation in the energy of the environment, can also indicate that dragons are manifesting.

The connection with dragons strengthens as the individual becomes more receptive and aware of these signs. Creating moments of introspection, whether through meditation, intuitive writing, or contemplation of nature, can facilitate this perception. Furthermore, honoring this presence with respect and genuine intention is essential to establishing a true bond. Dragons do not communicate in a linear way, but rather through impressions, feelings, and symbols that require careful interpretation. Those who dedicate themselves to this journey discover that dragons not only observe and guide from a distance, but also become powerful allies, offering protection, inspiration, and strength to navigate life's challenges with courage and purpose.

The signs of this return can manifest in different ways. Many people report a sudden interest in dragons, without any apparent reason. This call can come in the form of intense dreams, recurring images, synchronicities, and even a sense of familiarity when hearing stories about these beings. Some people begin to perceive dragons in everyday symbols, such as in natural patterns, clouds, or even in artistic manifestations that previously did not attract their attention. This indicates that their consciousness is opening up to this energy and that the dragons are trying to establish subtle contact.

Perceiving these signs requires sensitivity and attention. In everyday life, the draconic presence can reveal itself through small details that, to the distracted mind, would go unnoticed. Unexpected sounds, changes in ambient temperature, and even a feeling of inexplicable strength arising in moments of introspection can be indicative that dragons are near. Some people report feeling a watchful presence, as if they were being guided by an invisible force that encourages them to continue evolving. This type of experience can occur during meditations, moments of deep silence, or even in situations of great need, when a surge of courage arises seemingly out of nowhere.

Dreams and visions are some of the most common ways in which dragons come into contact with those who are awakening to their presence. In dreams, dragons may appear as grandiose figures, conveying symbolic messages or simply demonstrating their strength and majesty. Some people report telepathic dialogues with dragons, in which they receive guidance on their spiritual journey. Others describe the sensation of flying alongside a dragon, symbolizing freedom, elevation of consciousness, and overcoming limitations. The impact of these experiences is often profound, leaving a lasting impression and a sense of inexplicable connection with these beings.

The correct interpretation of these manifestations is essential to understanding the message that dragons wish to convey. Not every experience involving dragons indicates a genuine connection; sometimes, it can just be a manifestation of the unconscious processing powerful archetypes. To differentiate a real contact from a simple internal reflection, it is necessary to observe the impact of the experience. Authentic contacts with dragons usually bring significant changes in the perception of life, providing greater clarity, courage, and a renewed sense of purpose. Furthermore, these experiences are generally accompanied by a strong feeling of respect and admiration, rather than fear or confusion.

Strengthening this connection involves consciously opening oneself to the presence of dragons and demonstrating receptivity to their teachings. Focused meditations, respectful invocations, and visualization practices are effective ways to align personal energy with the draconic vibration. Creating a sacred space, be it a symbolic altar or a specific place for reflection and connection, can facilitate this attunement. Some practitioners also use crystals, such as obsidian and golden quartz, to amplify this energy and create a field more receptive to the presence of dragons.

The accounts of people who have felt the presence of dragons in their lives are varied, but they all share a common element: the profound transformation that this connection provides. Some people notice subtle changes, such as an increase in confidence and determination, while others go through true spiritual awakenings, where the draconic energy acts as a catalyst for their evolution. There are also those who report a continuous feeling of protection, as if they were being guided by an ancestral force that helps them face challenges and make important decisions.

The return of dragons to the consciousness of humanity is not an isolated event, but part of a larger process of reconnection with ancient forces that have always been present, but that have been dormant for a time. As more people awaken to this presence, the influence of dragons becomes more noticeable, guiding humanity towards a new era of understanding, power, and balance. Those who feel this call must be willing to delve into this journey, not as a search for power or superficial knowledge, but as a genuine commitment to their own growth and the expansion of consciousness.

Chapter 30
The Masters and Guardians

Dragons have always been more than mere symbols of strength and mystery; they represent spiritual masters who guide those willing to face the challenges of the evolutionary journey. Their presence in ancient traditions suggests that, beyond being guardians of sacred knowledge, they are rigorous instructors who test the determination and courage of those seeking wisdom. Unlike other spiritual entities that offer direct guidance and unconditional protection, dragons demand commitment and genuine transformation. The learning they provide isn't conveyed through gentle words or simple teachings, but through challenges that force the disciple to overcome their own limitations and achieve a deeper understanding of themselves and the universe.

This master-apprentice relationship is built on principles of merit and resilience. Dragons do not choose their students randomly; they observe the conduct, intention, and effort of each seeker. To be worthy of draconic guidance, one must demonstrate discipline, willpower, and a sincere search for self-knowledge. The teachings of dragons are often transmitted symbolically, through dreams, visions, and experiences that, at first glance, may seem challenging or enigmatic. These tests are not punishments, but opportunities for the individual to prove their determination and refine their spiritual abilities. Only those who are willing to face their own shadows and limitations can access the secrets that these guardians keep under their protection.

Draconic tutelage is not a shield that protects against all of life's difficulties, but a force that strengthens the spirit and broadens the perception of reality. Those who become attuned to dragons often report a profound transformation, feeling more secure, determined, and aligned with their purpose. This presence can be subtle, perceived as a heightened intuition or a surge of courage in the most crucial moments. Others experience more intense manifestations, such as vivid dreams in which dragons appear as masters teaching important lessons. Regardless of the form it takes, this connection is a call to constant evolution, challenging the individual to grow and become the best version of themselves. To work with dragons is to tread a path of power and responsibility, where each lesson learned translates into a firm step towards the awakening of true wisdom.

Throughout history, spiritual seekers have reported experiences that indicate the presence of dragons as hidden guides. In ancient texts, there are mentions of dragons as guardians of invisible temples, where only those who demonstrate true merit can enter. In some cultures, dragons were seen as protectors of the earth, knowledge, and the secrets of the universe. Taoist monks in China believed that dragons were manifestations of the primordial energy of the cosmos, capable of revealing paths to those who aligned themselves with their vibration. In the West, medieval alchemists used the image of the dragon as a symbol of the transmutation process, representing the apprentice's journey in search of enlightenment.

Access to the teachings of dragons does not occur randomly. It requires discipline, respect, and, above all, the ability to open oneself to profound changes. Dragons do not offer easy answers; instead, they present situations that force the practitioner to grow, overcome limitations, and reach new levels of consciousness. This transmission of knowledge can occur through dreams, visions, synchronicities, and even challenges in the physical world that serve as tests to strengthen the apprentice's soul. For those who are prepared, dragons offer keys to accessing higher dimensions of wisdom, expanding the perception of reality.

Draconic tutelage is a concept that refers to the spiritual protection and guidance granted by dragons to those who demonstrate that they are ready to walk beside them. This energetic protection can be felt as an invisible force that accompanies the individual in moments of danger or uncertainty. Many people who connect with dragons report feeling their presence when facing difficult situations, like a subtle energy that encourages them to move forward, strengthening their determination and mental clarity. This tutelage is not given indiscriminately; it must be earned through commitment to truth, integrity, and the pursuit of self-knowledge.

The accounts of people who have experienced this connection vary, but there are patterns that repeat. Some describe intense physical sensations when invoking the presence of dragons, such as a sudden warmth running through the body or a subtle electricity around the energy field. Others report recurring dreams in which dragons appear as teachers, leading them through unknown landscapes and revealing symbolic lessons. There are also those who perceive changes in their own energy after establishing this connection, feeling more confident, protected, and aligned with their life purpose.

Dragons, as masters and guardians, represent the raw force of cosmic wisdom, demanding from those who seek them a real and profound transformation. To work with their energy means abandoning illusions, facing painful truths, and, above all, developing a sense of responsibility for one's own spiritual journey. They do not guide those who expect easy answers or shortcuts to growth; instead, they offer challenges that lead to true awakening. For those who accept this call, the journey alongside dragons becomes a path of constant evolution, where each lesson learned strengthens not only the spirit, but also the very essence of being.

Chapter 31
The Final Calling

The connection with dragons transcends mere belief or mythological fascination. It's a transformative experience demanding commitment, keen perception, and a genuine willingness to change. Throughout this journey, each step taken has been not just a quest for the unknown, but a path of self-discovery, shaping the spirit and challenging the limitations imposed by fear and doubt. Those who reach this point do not arrive by chance. There's an inner drive, an undeniable force that has guided them here, overcoming obstacles, redefining paradigms, and allowing the blossoming of an expanded consciousness. It's not just about seeking dragons as external entities, but about recognizing the draconic essence within – that spark of power, wisdom, and strength that has been present from the beginning, awaiting the right moment to fully manifest.

The final calling is not just an invitation; it's a challenge. It's not enough to desire a connection with dragons; you must prove that you are ready to receive them. They don't respond to mere curiosity or superficial intentions, for their presence demands preparation, maturity, and the courage to face truths that may be uncomfortable. Each person who treads this path must ask themselves: Am I willing to abandon old illusions? Do I have the courage to face the challenges that lie ahead? The presence of a dragon is not a gift granted without purpose; it's a reflection of what has been earned, of the clarity that has been developed, and of the inner strength that has solidified throughout the journey. Therefore, those who hesitate, who doubt, or who still carry emotional and mental baggage will find it difficult to proceed. The true encounter with dragons happens only when there is a total surrender to the process of transformation, without reservation or resistance.

The signs of readiness are everywhere for those who have learned to see them. Vivid dreams where dragons manifest, unexpected synchronicities, a profound shift in the perception of reality – all these are indications that draconic energy is drawing near. But the most important thing is not outside, but within: an inexplicable feeling that something grand is about to happen, an awakening that echoes in the soul and resonates with an unquestionable truth. This is the final calling. Now, only the decision remains. Are you ready to take the next step and cross the threshold that separates what was and what can yet be?

Dragons are not entities that appear by chance. Their energy cannot simply be invoked by desire or momentary need. They emerge for those who demonstrate that they are prepared to receive their teachings and to deal with the responsibilities that come with this connection. Many spiritual traditions speak of the importance of spiritual maturity before approaching beings of great power. In the case of dragons, this preparation involves more than just rituals and invocations; it requires a change in the way one perceives reality and interacts with the world.

Readiness for this encounter is not measured solely by accumulated knowledge, but by the willingness to abandon old limiting beliefs and embrace the unknown with courage. Dragons challenge those who seek them to become more authentic versions of themselves, demanding integrity, determination, and an unwavering commitment to the truth. They don't offer easy paths or ready-made answers, but place the individual before challenges that force them to grow, to strengthen themselves, and to expand their consciousness.

The signs that someone is ready for an encounter with dragons are subtle, but clear to those who learn to observe them. One of the first indications is the constant presence of synchronicities involving dragons – whether through images, unexpected mentions in conversations, or even repetitive dreams where these beings appear. These manifestations suggest that draconic energy is approaching, testing the individual's level of receptivity. Furthermore, there is a perceptible internal transformation: a growing desire to break free from destructive patterns, a deep yearning to understand hidden mysteries, and a renewed courage to face challenges that once seemed insurmountable.

For those who feel this calling, preparation becomes essential. Meditations focused on the energy of dragons, practices of energy alignment, and in-depth study of their symbology are ways to strengthen this connection. But, above all, it is necessary to cultivate a spirit of respect and humility. Dragons do not respond to arrogance or the pursuit of personal power; they manifest for those who wish to understand themselves and the universe in a deeper way.

The encounter with a dragon, whether in a dream, in a vision, or in an intense spiritual experience, is not something that can be forced. It happens when the soul is ready, when the mind is open, and when the heart is free of rigid expectations. Many people report that when they finally encountered a dragon, it was not in the way they expected. Some described an immense and indescribable presence, which felt like a wave of heat or electricity coursing through their body. Others saw the dragons as imposing and serene figures, communicating through symbols, gazes, or deep sensations. There are those who only felt a force around them, like an invisible shield that protected them in moments of crisis.

Regardless of the form the encounter takes, it always provokes change. Whoever comes into contact with a true dragon never sees life the same way again. Fear dissipates, perception expands, and a new sense of purpose sets in. This doesn't mean the journey becomes easy, but that the individual now has a powerful ally at their side, a force that inspires them to keep growing, learning, and facing challenges with wisdom and determination.

The calling of dragons is not for everyone. It resonates only with those who are ready to accept its grandeur and the challenges it brings. If you feel this connection, if dragons populate your thoughts, dreams, and intuitions, then perhaps you are already prepared for the encounter. But remember: this is not the end of the journey, but the beginning of a new phase, where the draconic presence will become a constant guide, propelling your evolution to levels you can't even imagine yet.

Now, the decision is in your hands. Are you ready to answer the call?

Epilogue

I would like to express my sincerest gratitude to you, dear reader, for dedicating your time and attention to this deep exploration of the true nature of dragons. We hope that this journey through the pages of this book has awakened your curiosity, expanded your understanding, and, perhaps, even touched a sensitive fiber in your soul.

We believe that the pursuit of knowledge and openness to new perspectives are essential paths for our individual and collective growth. By allowing yourself to consider the possibility that dragons are more than mere figures of mythology, you demonstrate an open mind and a thirst to understand the deeper layers of reality.

The realization of this book was possible thanks to the effort and dedication of many people. On behalf of the author, I would like to thank all those who contributed directly or indirectly to this project. We especially thank those who shared their experiences and insights about the subtle world and the presence of dragons, enriching this work with their personal experiences.

We would also like to acknowledge the tireless work of the editorial team, who, with professionalism and attention to detail, made this book a reality. We thank the proofreaders, designers, and everyone involved in the production, whose expertise was essential to shape these words and make them accessible to you.

Finally, a special thanks to those who, with their support and encouragement, motivated the author to continue with this research and share his unique vision of dragons.

We sincerely hope that reading this book has been an enriching and inspiring experience, and that the information presented here can serve as a starting point for an even deeper journey in search of understanding our connection with the spiritual world and the elemental forces that govern it.

May the wisdom of dragons, beings of power and transformation, continue to inspire your thoughts and illuminate your path.

With best wishes,
Luiz Santos Editor

www.ingramcontent.com/pod-product-compliance
Lightning Source LLC
LaVergne TN
LVHW040054080526
838202LV00045B/3636